RESHAPING CHRISTIAN IDENTITY

ENCOUNTERING JESUS IN LUKE

RESHAPING CHRISTIAN IDENTITY: ENCOUNTERING JESUS IN LUKE

ISBN 978-1-329-77521-3

RESHAPING CHRISTIAN IDENTITY

ENCOUNTERING JESUS IN LUKE

BRAD T BROMLING

A Doctoral Dissertation as submitted to (and approved by) the faculties of the schools of the Atlanta Theological Association in partial fulfillment of the requirements for the degree of Doctor of Ministry at Columbia Theological Seminary.

DEDICATION

I dedicate
this project to
Kimberly Bromling,
my wife, friend, and fellow traveler.
You have inspired, challenged, and walked with me.
Your patience and encouragement made it possible for me to
believe I could finish the project after it was derailed and
seemed too daunting to complete.

TABLE OF CONTENTS

CHAPTER 1
AN IDENTITY CRISIS

Bob's Story

Eighteen years ago, when Bob was baptized, he was confident he was doing the right thing. He had studied diligently and knew what he believed. His life was filled with purpose; he had a sense of direction and security. He looked forward to attending church services and never entertained the thought of intentionally missing a worship service or prayer meeting. He was proud to be a member of the church he read about in the Bible —the Church of Christ. The sense that he was standing on solid ground was strong for seven or eight years. He talked about the church to his friends, invited his co-workers to Gospel Meetings, and even knocked on doors in the community with the preacher.

Then things began to change. It was gradual at first, but in time it became more and more difficult for him to make sense of what he believed. Now Bob is frustrated and confused. He does not know what to do or where to go. He is sick of the "issues." There have been so many that have gotten the church stirred up that he can't remember them all. A few stand out, though. The first issue was whether the church could operate a "Joy Bus" to bring in children from the community. "There's no authority for busses!" was the voice that prevailed. Bob was disappointed to see the church across town start a bus program in such clear violation of biblical authority.

Before long, the matter of using new translations of the Bible became the issue. The church had always used the King James Version. It was the version that was read from the pulpit and the one the preacher always quoted. Then some of the members requested that the elders replace the tattered pew Bibles with New International Version Bibles. In response, the elders asked the preacher to present a series of sermons on "the danger of modern versions." By the time he finished the eighth lesson in the series, four families were gone (they went to another congregation that didn't place as high a premium on "truth" in such matters —at least that's what the preacher said). The elders mailed a letter to every member of the congregation that said while they were free to use whatever version they wanted in their personal study at home, only the King James Version and the American Standard Version of 1901 would be allowed in the public assemblies of the church. They also replaced the worn pew Bibles with King James Bibles. Bob struggled with this issue. After all, he had been using the New American Standard Version for a few years and appreciated its clarity. Although he did not agree completely, he complied with the wishes of the elders.

The next issue to blaze hotly across the city was whether it was scriptural for Churches of Christ to use a denominational film series in its assemblies. The big downtown church had sent out a letter to all the area churches inviting them to attend a special showing of the James Dobson films in their building. The preacher at Bob's congregation made the mistake of reading the announcement from the pulpit. The elders were livid. When they questioned him and discovered he didn't have a problem with it, they fired him! A few more families left. Bob didn't like the way the matter was handled, but agreed with the elders' logic.

After a while, the "issues" began to run together: is social drinking a sin?; is it wrong to use instrumental music in worship?; should women wear pants in church services?; must men wear suits to wait on the Lord's Table?; must an elder have more than one child?; is it Scriptural to clap when someone is baptized?; etc. It seemed that all the preachers and elders wanted to discuss had to do with what was wrong with this church or that preacher.

Bob has always felt strongly about the Bible's authority, so it has been easy for him to take sides in many of the controversies; but what has been eating away at his soul little by little has been a sense of emptiness. For a while, he attributed it to his wife's death. Five years ago she died of cancer. Her absence left him lonely, to be sure, but enough time has now passed for him to be able to distinguish between loneliness and the spiritual emptiness that is bothering him. He used to be so excited about doing things with the church; but it has been months since he looked forward to meeting with the church. Oh, he's always there, he just doesn't see the point anymore. He doesn't know what to do. He is tired of his congregation's preoccupation with "issues," but knows there is nowhere else to go. After all, the other Churches of Christ are compromised in various ways and the denominational churches don't seem to respect the authority of the Bible at all.

“What am I going to do?” Bob asked himself as he stood pumping gas. Suddenly, his thoughts were interrupted by a familiar voice: “Hey Bob, how are you doing?”

Bob, feeling a bit startled, turned to see his neighbor Larry returning to his truck after paying for his gas. Bob cleared his throat and responded with a somewhat tentative “I’m fine; how are you?”

“I’m doing well,” Larry answered. He sensed the discordant note in Bob’s voice and said, “Say, my wife’s gone to her sister’s this week and I’m baching it. I’ve got some great steaks in the 'fridge, why not come over tonight?”

Bob wanted to say yes, but tried to refuse. “Thanks, but I better pass; I’m sure you’ve got other things to do. Maybe some other time.”

“I would really like for you to come; I’m getting pretty tired of sitting around by myself. Besides, if I don’t eat those steaks, I’ll have to throw them out,” Larry said. He sounded genuine. Bob thought for a second and realized that he could use some company himself.

“Are you sure?”

“Of course!”

"All right, but let me pick up the drinks; O.K.?”

“Fair enough. I’ll see you at 6:30,” Larry said with a smile. He got into his truck and drove off.

Bob paid for his gas, picked up a couple six-packs of Coke and headed home. As he drove, he thought about Larry. They had known each other for a long time, but they hadn’t been very close. Larry was a member of a denominational church, so Bob had kept his distance. He was always one of the first people Bob invited when his congregation conducted Gospel Meetings; Larry had even come once to hear a speech about Creation and Evolution. Bob had never accepted any of Larry’s invitations to go to his church’s special services, though. Bob felt badly about that, but he couldn’t see how he could go to a church that didn’t preach “sound doctrine.”

When Bob arrived, Larry was ready to put the steaks on the grill. They engaged in a good bit of small talk while the meat was cooking, then they sat down to eat. When the silence was sustained for a few moments, Larry carefully broached the subject of church. “Bob,” he said, “I’ve known you for a long time. All that time you have been a member of the same church. I’ve seen you helping out around there a lot, and whenever they have a revival, I can count on you to knock on my door. But, I just realized that I don't really know anything about your church. Tell me, what does the Church of Christ believe?"

Bob felt his ears burn as he swallowed a bite of potato and tried to decide where to start with his answer. "Well, we believe the Bible is the inspired Word of God and that it is our only authority in all religious matters," Bob said.

"Don't all churches believe that?" Larry asked, sounding somewhat puzzled.

"Not really; most have some book besides to Bible that tells them what they believe —creed books and confessions," Bob responded. "Take the Baptists, for instance, they follow a Manual that lists their major beliefs."

"But aren't those beliefs simply principles drawn from the pages of the Bible?" Larry asked, sounding even more confused.

"No; the Bible only makes Christians, it takes Baptist creeds to make a Baptist," Bob said flatly. He then proceeded to explain why the Church of Christ doesn't use a piano in its worship, and why its preachers aren't called "pastor." Point by point he told Larry how the Church of Christ differed from the other churches and answered Larry's questions about its distinctive doctrines. After more than an hour of talking, both men tired of the subject. Bob felt he had been on the hot seat, and Larry's head was swimming.

"Do all Churches of Christ believe those things?" Larry asked.

"The ones that are faithful do; there are some that are liberal and don't follow the Bible like they should," Bob answered.

"Who decides which ones are faithful?" Larry asked.

Bob paused for a moment and said, "All of us do. I mean, if a church does something that is not in the Bible, we know it is not faithful."

Larry smiled and said, "That's all very interesting. You've told me some things I didn't know. I read the Bible a lot; I just missed that stuff. I'll have to go back and do some more study."

They talked about the weather and work, and eventually said good-bye. As Bob walked home he felt frustrated. He had said so much, and yet he wondered if he had said the right things. As he replayed the conversation in his mind he thought how hollow some of the answers he gave sounded.

"Do I really believe this stuff, anymore?" he wondered as he fell into bed.

Bob is an average member of the Church of Christ. Although he doesn't yet know how to articulate it, he is suffering from an identity crisis.[1] He has always defined his Christianity according to the Church of Christ's distinctive doctrines —the kind of things he told Larry. Yet, as he reflects on the way his congregation has struggled with issue after issue, he feels a nagging emptiness in his heart. "Isn't there more to being a Christian, than being right about these issues?" he often asks himself.

The Church of Christ teaches that it is the one true church built by Jesus Christ on the first Pentecost after his resurrection and ascension. It affirms that since the church was corrupted by Catholicism, and only partially restored by Protestantism, it continued in a state of apostasy until the early decades of the 19th Century. The Church credits men like Thomas and Alexander Campbell with recognizing the need to search for the "ancient order" and to restore the New Testament Church. Its plea is for non-denominational Christianity, based upon "no creed but Christ, and no book but the Bible." The Church contends that to be faithful, Christians must "speak where the Bible speaks, and be silent where the Bible is silent." This means that they will "call Bible things by Bible names and do Bible things in Bible ways." The Church considers itself to be made up of "people of the Book" and takes pride in its history of powerful debaters and "Book-chapter-and-verse" preachers.[2]

In the century-and-a-half since the Campbells, Christian identity in the Church of Christ has been reckoned, essentially, according to one's adherence to the Church's distinctive doctrines. The Church has been known more for what it does not believe (i.e., for its opposition to mechanical instruments of music in worship, infant baptism, women preachers, and many other such things), than for what it affirms about the saving message of Jesus Christ. It is commonplace for members of the Church of Christ to be asked two questions: "Aren't you the group that doesn't believe in music?" and "Is it true that you think you are the only ones going to heaven?"

Unfortunately, what has been missing, to a large extent, is emphasis upon the person of Jesus Christ. Jesus is certainly taught as being the Son of God who died to take away the sin of the world. Although the Church does have a rather high Christology, it does not intentionally deny any biblical teaching about Jesus. Jesus is held up as the supreme example of self-giving love and moral purity. He is exalted, at least in song, as King of kings and Lord of lords. The Church concludes all its prayers "in Jesus' name", and baptizes "in the name of the Father, Son, and Holy Ghost." The biblical designation "Church of Christ" is used in order to honor Christ as the head of the Church. While all of these things are true, and while the Church of Christ would never intentionally say or teach anything that would detract from Jesus Christ, nonetheless, it still tends to derive its identity as a community (and as individuals) from its doctrinal distinctiveness and not from its relationship to its Savior.

This method of reckoning Christian identity is deficient. Theologically, it short-changes the grace of God and fosters a system of justification by works. It tends to be divisive, and is powerless to transform individuals into the image of Jesus Christ. In an age when denominational loyalties cannot be taken for granted, many members of the Church of Christ seem less concerned about the Church's distinctiveness and more concerned about having a faith that is relevant in the face of everyday pressures. This deficiency is responsible for the sense of emptiness that Bob and so many others like him in the Church of Christ are feeling. There are several signs indicating that the Church of Christ has an institutional, rather than a christological, center for its identity.

One of the more obvious signs relates to the Church's approach to evangelism. The bare essentials of the plan of salvation (hear, believe, repent, confess, and be baptized) are often printed on church stationery, flyers announcing church functions, and even on business cards used by its preachers. In this way, the Church attempts to send a clear message that its teaching about how one becomes a Christian is correct. The problem is, to people who are unfamiliar with the Church of Christ, this method tells them virtually nothing about either their need for Jesus or his desire and ability to save them. It is a presentation of "the plan," but not "the Man." The common personal work tools (filmstrips, flip charts, correspondence courses) used by the Church of Christ are also largely deficient in this area. The usual strategy is to explain the over-all plan of the Bible, point out that the Old Testament laws have been superseded by the New Law of Christ, and to show what Jesus commands people to do in order to be saved. While some time is spent explaining the vicarious nature of Jesus' suffering on the cross and his victory over death in resurrection, the main thrust is upon encouraging an understanding that Jesus has the right to specify the conditions of salvation and explaining what those conditions are.

When Bob was baptized, he did so in humble obedience to a biblical requirement. In his mind (and through his action) he acknowledged that Jesus had the authority to make such a demand. Although he did not believe his baptism was a meritorious work sufficient to save him, he did view it as an act of obedience apart from which he could not be saved. His focus was not upon the finished work of Jesus upon the cross, but upon the obedient response he was making to the offer of salvation. Even at this crucial beginning point in his Christian life, Jesus was more of a historical figure than a present reality. While in theory Bob accepted that Jesus continues to live in heaven, in practical terms he conceived of Jesus as having lived and worked in the distant past to make salvation possible.

Another sign of the problematic approach is seen in the issues that divide conscientious members of the Church. Because the emphasis is upon doctrinal distinctions, it is not inconceivable to see congregations split over such controversies as modern Bible translations, church support of Christian colleges, or whether it is appropriate to applaud after a baptism. Since the common ground for church members is sought upon doctrine, any variation of opinion in doctrine is potentially divisive. Bob had seen many fellow-Christians leave his home congregation for another across town because of various "doctrinal" issues. Most of the time he was unsympathetic toward them because it seemed that the ones who left did so out of a spirit of rebellion to the plain truth of Scripture. To him, it looked as though they were more concerned with doing things that suited themselves than with doing what the Scriptures authorized. He lost some friends in this way, as well. He felt pity for them and hoped they would repent; but he was sure that many of them simply did not love the Truth enough to stay with the faithful.

Yet another sign is the Church's silence about Jesus Christ. Aside from its liturgical use in worship, the name of Jesus is rarely heard among the members of this community of faith. As a rule, Jesus' presence in the Christian life is largely unacknowledged. This is not only true when members of the church interact with non-Christians, but mention of Jesus is equally absent when members talk with other members. Bob had often shared meals with visiting preachers. More often than not the topic of discussion surrounded the doctrinal positions of this or that preacher. Bob could not remember a time when he was asked by a preacher about his relationship with Jesus. Although he always assumed that these preachers had a daily walk with Jesus, he cannot remember a time when any of the preachers spoke of their relationship with the Savior. There were always plenty of controversial issues to discuss, instead.

Since many people in the Church of Christ think it is unscriptural to pray to Jesus, even times of distress are endured with scarcely a thought of Jesus. (Needless to say, "Have a little talk with Jesus" is an unwelcome song in some congregations.)

When Bob's wife Molly died, he cherished the outpouring of love shown to him by the members of his congregation. They brought a lot of food, sent several cards, and told him often that they were praying for him. These expressions of concern touched him, and he was bolstered by them. But in his bed, when he cried out in the night, he found it difficult to feel the presence of God (and certainly, an awareness of the presence of Jesus was wholly absent). In Bob's theology, God is so high and holy (and Jesus is so chronologically and spatially distant), that Bob has always found it hard to see how his faith makes much difference in suffering. Fortunately, the fact that Molly was a Christian keeps him safely back from the brink of despair. But sometimes, while melancholy and alone, Bob wonders if anyone ever really feels close to God. "Maybe that's reserved for heaven," he said to himself as he turned out the light above his bed.

The Project

It is my conviction that members of the Church of Christ like Bob, must learn to reshape their individual (and, in turn, corporate) Christian identities christologically (that is, according to their encounter with the person of Jesus Christ). This is a crucial area of concern because a person who has an inadequate or confused Christian identity is incapable of bearing a faithful witness of Christ to the world and of finding the power to live the faith he or she professes.

The Act of Ministry that I am proposing is the writing of a study guide-type adult class book on the subject of reshaping Christian identity christologically. The class book will consist of eight chapters (to be taught over an eight week period). I will define the parameters, methodology, and goals of such a class book. I will then propose an outline of the book's chapters and show how the book will identify the crisis and address the issue through a study of specific narratives contained in Luke-Acts. The book will ask and answer the questions: What is the identity of Jesus in Luke-Acts and in what ways might our encounter with the Lukan Jesus reshape our identity?

The proposed project will stand upon a synthesis of three areas of research: Christology; Narrative Theology; and Luke-Acts. Since I am proposing that Christian identity should be shaped christologically, a basic understanding of how the church has struggled to understand the identity of Jesus Christ would be helpful (Chapter 2).

Narrative theology is crucial to this study because of the insights it offers relative to the shaping of personal identity and the way the gospel, as story, impacts our lives (Chapter 3). We are, after all, story beings living in a story world who are guided by the stories of Scripture. Narrative encounters provide occasions for men and women to be changed.

Luke-Acts provides the specific textual environment for the project (Chapter 4). As an example of narrative theology, Luke-Acts enables us to encounter Jesus in an identity-shaping way. Luke-Acts presents us with a portrait of Jesus as universal savior whose ministry of seeking after and saving the lost was intended to benefit each of us, and to challenge every distortion of humanity that sin has caused (e.g., dysfunctional human relationships, self-destructive behavior, and separation from fellowship with the Creator).

CHAPTER 2

CHRISTOLOGY AND CHRISTIAN IDENTITY

Introduction

"I have been crucified with Christ; and it is no longer I who live, but it is Christ who lives in me. And the life I now live in the flesh I live by faith in the Son of God, who loved me and gave Himself for me" (Galatians 2:19b-20).[3] These striking words point to the relationship between Christology and Christian identity.[4] To be a Christian implies two distinct conclusions regarding personal identity: something dies and something else lives in its place. For Paul, the thing that died was his "old" self and the thing that lived in its place was "Christ" (Romans 6:6; Colossians 1:27). In other words, when Paul encountered Jesus of Nazareth his personal identity was so radically altered that he could only describe it in terms of death and new life (Romans 6:1-4). This meant that all he had previously counted as valuable was counted as worthless (Philippians 3:7). That which he had previously counted as worthless (and worthy of only persecution), came to be counted as of supreme value —the person whom he confessed as Christ. Paul calls the Church to see his experience as paradigmatic (1 Corinthians 11:1). This is not an arrogant expectation but an apparent reflection of the teaching of Jesus himself (Luke 9:23; 12:8-9). This is why Christian identity must be rooted in Christology. But what do we mean by "Christology"?

Christology means more than simply "a word about Christ" as the etymology of the term implies. It bears a heavier load. It is also more specific than merely "human reflection on the person of Christ" (Fuller & Perkins:1). Christology is the discipline of study that seeks to answer the question, "Who is this person who stands at the center of Christian faith?" (Guthrie: 230). As such, its task is even broader than simply "understanding how this man [Jesus of Nazareth —BTB] is God" (Pannenberg:31). John Macquarrie suggests that Christology is the third layer of one's consideration of Jesus. The first layer is the historical figure of Jesus —the rabbi who busied himself among the Jews of first-century Palestine. The second layer is "gospel", that is, the artistic presentation of Jesus and his significance to the earliest Christian communities. Christology, the third layer, is "gospel that has been subjected to reflection and criticism" (Macquarrie:16). Put in slightly different terms, then, Christology involves the threefold inquiry of: (1) seeking to know what can be known of the historical Jesus; (2) attempting to understand how "in Christ God was reconciling the world to himself" (2 Corinthians 5:19); and (3) reflecting on how this knowledge and understanding changes the life of the one who confesses that "Jesus is Lord" (Romans 10:9). So christological reflection has practical implications for the identity of those who bear the name Christian.

The Gospel of John portrays Jesus as saying, "Whoever has seen me has seen the Father" (John 14:9). In a similar way, the Christian community confesses, "Whoever has seen us has seen Jesus." To make this confession involves a reorienting of an individual's personal identity, to see and present one's self as an essentially different (new) person because of Jesus Christ.

In this project, "personal identity" refers to the way a man or woman defines and/or identifies (considers internally and displays externally) himself or herself. At issue is not the technical concern of psychology regarding the construction of a person's core identity, nor necessarily the way an individual is defined by others. Rather, the focus is on how an individual defines and manifests himself or herself after he or she has converted to Christianity. In the main, personal identity arises out of the interplay of three things: (1) one's actual life history (specifically one's memory of important events in that history); (2) one's place within one's social/cultural contexts (one's relationships and responsibilities); and (3) the interpretation of that history and social/cultural context (Stroup:101-118). Hans Frei has put it in these words: "A person's identity is the self-referral, or ascription to him [sic.] of his physical and personal states, properties, characteristics, and actions" (38).

There seems to be a strong expectation in Scripture that Christian conversion results in a transformation of personal identity (see 1 Corinthians 6:11; 2 Corinthians 5:17; and Galatians 6:15); that transformation occurs when one accepts the Christian worldview as the controlling factor for reinterpreting one's history and social/cultural context (Stroup:170-175). The thesis of this project is that the primary focus of that reinterpretation should be Jesus Christ, not the doctrines of a particular church. This chapter will briefly survey the way the Church has struggled to understand the identity of Jesus Christ and consider how that struggle influences the shaping of Christian identity.

New Testament Confessions

The twenty-seven books of the New Testament contain a significant amount of what is known about Jesus Christ. For Christians, the information these books provide is given favored status over the data gained from other sources (such as extra-canonical texts and personal experience). Whether taken alone or together, however, these books do not provide a systematic discourse on the person, nature, and work of Jesus Christ. Instead, they preserve the confessions of faith expressed by some of his earliest followers. While at times these confessions are the main focus of the individual book (e.g., Mark 1:1; John 20:30-21; Hebrews 1:1-2), they are at other times simply implied (e.g., Jude). In most cases, however, the confessions permeate the books because their authors were people of profound faith who could not imagine life without reference to Jesus (e.g., Romans 1:1; 1 Peter). Part of the role of Christology is to explore these texts, uncover the explicit and implicit claims they make regarding Jesus Christ, and ask how these claims impact the life of one who confesses "Jesus is Lord" (1 Corinthians 12:3). These claims are at times similar from text to text, and at other times quite dissimilar. Contemporary readers of the ancient texts must respect this diversity and hold the dissimilarities in tension, rather than feel compelled to choose one expression over all others (Dupuis:74-75). The differences do not amount to contradiction; they show instead that the early Christians found a variety of ways to express their faith, which is as true today as it was then. In order to demonstrate this diversity, the next section of this chapter will discuss briefly the Christology of the Gospels and Acts.

Christology in the Gospels and Acts

Although the twenty-one epistles that comprise almost half of the New Testament also contain important and diverse christological confessions and perspectives, this project will limit its scope to the first half of the New Testament. This will be sufficient to demonstrate some of the variety and similarity of ancient christological reflection.

The New Testament opens with four books that are primarily narrative in form, and have as their central focus the life, death, and resurrection of Jesus. They are called "Gospels" which is the English rendering of the Greek word euangelion, meaning "good news." Although these books originally circulated without titles, by the late second century C.E. the present titles were assigned to them. Because they tell the good news about Jesus, they each share the common title "The Gospel According to...." Their authors (often referred to as the "evangelists") tell this good news from decidedly different perspectives, emphasizing different aspects of the Jesus story and meeting theological concerns appropriate to the needs of their communities. It is easy for contemporary readers to miss this fact and to read the Gospels as though they were simply the same story, with different details. Read thusly, a forced harmony is constructed: their similar passages are collapsed into a singular record, their dissimilar passages are arranged "chronologically", and their conflicting passages are minimized, or ignored altogether. Gospel harmonization of this sort is nothing new; since as early as 155 C.E. Justin's disciple Tatian compiled his own harmony of the Gospels called the Diatessaron (literally "through the four"). While such a harmony is not completely bereft of value, the individual Gospels, as independent literary compositions, should be heard on their own —as indeed they were heard when first circulated among the early Christians. When carefully read, it is evident that each Gospel presents a particular mental picture of Jesus that differs in specific and important ways from the others. These differences point to the intriguing diversity of primitive Christian thought. Although not attempting to represent a scholarly consensus, the following summaries are offered to illustrate the kind of christological diversity that one encounters when allowing each Gospel to speak for itself.

The Christology of Matthew

The Gospel of Matthew functions as more than simply the first book of the New Testament; because of its Christology this Gospel serves as a crucial bridge connecting the two sections of the Christian Scriptures. The evangelist presents a Jesus who is at every step and turn fulfilling Scripture. Seemingly everything —from how his mother conceived him to how his clothing was distributed among the soldiers who crucified him — happened "to fulfill what had been spoken" by the prophets of Israel (Matthew 1:22; 2:15,17,23; 4:14; 5:18; 8:17; 12:17; 13:14,14,35; 21:14; 26:54,56; 27:9,35). This Jesus whose life the evangelist contends was predicted in detail by the prophets, is greater than the temple, greater than the prophet Jonah, and greater than king Solomon (12:6,41,42). He is in fact, greater even than Moses.

While Matthew portrays Jesus as a "Moses-like figure" (Fuller and Perkins:84) who shares some similarities with the great lawgiver (such as being threatened with infanticide, being called forth from Egypt by God, and delivering authoritative teaching from a "mount", et al. [2:13-21; 5:1]) it is clear that Jesus is superior to Moses. Jesus' authority/superiority is, in fact, more to the point of the evangelist's Christology. Magi travel from afar to pay him homage —even as an infant (2:1-12) —and a Roman officer calls himself unworthy to have Jesus step into his house (8:8). The wind and waves obey his voice (8:27), demonic legions tremble in his presence (8:29), and human diseases of all kinds are powerless in his presence (4:24). Jesus speaks with an audacious authority that amazes the crowds (7:28) and offends the religious leaders (15:12). Instead of quoting the great Rabbis, he often says, "I say to you" (fifty-four times in Matthew), showing no hesitation to correct erroneous applications of Old Testament Scripture (e.g., 5:28ff). "In the Sermon on the Mount. . . Jesus takes the position of God, not Moses" (Meier, 1992:637). It would be difficult to find anyone or anything over which Jesus does not have authority in Matthew. The only authority indisputably greater than his belongs to his heavenly father; even that seems to be delivered into his hands after his resurrection (28:18). The Jesus presented in Matthew is Emmanuel (i.e., "God is with us"), who promises to be among those gathered in his name and with his followers "always" (1:23; 18:20; 28:20).

Matthew's heavy emphasis upon Jesus' superiority may be a response to the pressure exerted upon the evangelist's community by the Jewish leaders who, in the wake of Jerusalem's fall (70 C.E.), apparently gathered in the Roman town of Yavneh to establish Pharisaic Judaism as normative. It seems these leaders sought to unify Judaism and delegitimize all competing sects, including Jewish Christianity (Fuller and Perkins:81-86; Overman:38-43). Matthew's response is, "Jesus' authority exceeds everything else —no matter what the leaders of Yavneh say." This picture of Jesus makes significant claims on Matthew's community: as a body its authority was to be found in the Gospel; as individuals, their identity as Christians was shaped by the example and ethics of this one who possessed "all authority."

The Christology of Mark

The Gospel of Mark opens with these words: "The beginning of the good news of Jesus Christ, the Son of God." Jesus is thus immediately assigned two designations: "Christ" (literally, "the anointed one" —Christ is the Greek parallel to the Hebrew "messiah"); and, "Son of God." The evangelist skillfully weaves them both into the fabric of his Gospel and reveals their meanings within key narrative scenes. When Jesus asked his disciples, "But who do you say that I am?" Peter answered: "You are the Messiah" (Mark 8:29). At his trial, Jesus is asked if he is "the Messiah." He responds "I am" (14:62). While he hangs on the cross, the religious leaders sarcastically call him "the Messiah" (15:32).

What does it mean for Jesus to be the Christ/Messiah? It certainly differed from what the Jewish leaders thought. Although they held tenaciously to a messianic hope —perhaps expecting both a messianic king and a messianic priest (O'Collins:26) —Mark contends that (contrary to their expectations) their hope was fulfilled in the man whom they sentenced to die on a cross! Jesus wasn't crucified in spite of his messiahship, but because of it. Mark intentionally links messiahship with suffering (which is reminiscent of Isaiah 53; cf. Acts 8:34-35).

When Peter reaches the point where he can confess Jesus as Messiah, Jesus begins to warn his followers of his approaching death (8:29,31). Although no one understands its significance, Jesus continues to stress that he will be killed and raised (9:30-32; 10:32-34; 12:1-12; 14:8). Whatever Mark intended to convey in calling Jesus "Christ" he links it to death on the cross.

The designation "Son of God" is applied to Jesus five times in Mark (six counting Jesus' reference to God as "Abba Father" —14:36): twice it is said by demons (3:11; 5:7); twice it is said by God (1:11; 9:7); once it is spoken by a centurion who witnessed the death of Jesus (15:39). There seems to be some significance in the fact that although the reader is told up front that Jesus is the "Son of God" no human voice expresses this evaluation until the crucifixion; that one human voice belongs to a Gentile (who has neither seen Jesus' miracles nor heard any of his authoritative teaching)! Why don't Peter and the disciples confess it (as they do in Matthew 14:33; 16:16)? Why don't John the Baptist, Nathanael, and Martha confess it (as they do in John 1:34, 49; 11:27)? Apparently, Mark has a point to make. It appears that he is trying to say, "Jesus could only be accurately seen as the Messiah, Son of God, in view of his death on the cross" (Guelich:16; Stroup:160).

Mark is in a hurry to show us the cross; and what is it that we see there? Not a criminal, but a king (Achtemeier:551-553). Like the ancient Israelite kings, Jesus is the "anointed" "Son of God" (cf. Mark 15:32 and Psalm 2:2; Mark 1:11 and Psalm 2:7). According to Mark, Jesus is the anointed king whose identity is finally revealed in his crucifixion. This perspective possibly served two important purposes for the evangelist's community. First, it flew in the face of the false messiahs who were troubling the evangelist's community (Fuller and Perkins:67-77). The true Messiah is the one who died on the cross; he isn't, therefore, among those purporting to work amazing acts to gather a following (Mark 13:21-22). Second, it defined Christian discipleship. As Stroup contends:

> The genius of Mark's Gospel is that it is impossible to read it, agree with the [centurion's] confession "`Truly this man was the Son of God'" (Mark 15:39) and then ask what discipleship means. The reader

> may find the answer to that question unpleasant or unacceptable but Mark leaves little doubt what discipleship means. (163)

For the Markan community, to be a disciple is to follow the Master's path of taking up the cross: living a life of self-sacrifice and being a servant of all.

The Christology of Luke-Acts

Although not printed in immediate succession in our New Testaments, the Gospel According to Luke and the Acts of the Apostles generally are considered the work of the same hand that are to be read as two parts of the same narrative (Johnson, 1992:404). The themes introduced in the Gospel are picked up and carried forward by the Acts (see Acts 1:1). As such, it is possible to speak of the Christology of Luke-Acts as a unit. The focus of Lukan Christology seems best summarized in the title "Savior." Dumbfounded shepherds are told by angelic visitors, "to you is born this day in the city of David a Savior, who is the Messiah, the Lord" (Luke 2:11). Earlier, at the birth of Jesus' forerunner, John, his father Zechariah prophesied, "[God] has raised up a mighty savior for us in the house of his servant David" (1:69) and claimed that this fulfilled the promises God made to Abraham. In Luke-Acts, the story of Jesus and his church is of one piece with the salvation history of Abraham's descendants. What God promised in the Old Testament, Jesus began to fulfill in Luke and continued to fulfill in the Acts —namely, universal salvation (Fuller and Perkins:86-92). This emphasis on salvation recurs throughout the narrative. The aged Simeon is told by the Holy Spirit that he would not die until he saw "the Lord's Messiah" (2:26); when he sees the baby Jesus he exclaims:

> Master, now you are dismissing your servant in peace, according to your word; for my eyes have seen your salvation, which you have prepared in the presence of all peoples, a light for the revelation to the Gentiles and for glory to your people Israel. (2:29-32)

Simeon recognized Jesus as the Messiah, the one through whom God's promised salvation would come.

To describe the ministry of John, the evangelist draws upon the language of Isaiah 40:

> The voice of one crying out in the wilderness: Prepare the way of the Lord; make his paths straight. Every valley shall be filled, and every mountain and hill shall be made low, and the crooked shall be made straight, and the rough ways made smooth. (Luke 3:4-5)

All this preparation culminates in the ultimate goal: "and all flesh shall see the salvation of God" (3:6). John "prepared the way" so that in Jesus humanity could experience salvation. Through his ministry Jesus begins offering the salvation of God to all people regardless of their ethnic stock, economic status, social standing, religious purity, or gender. Jesus fraternizes with social outcasts (19:5), eats with sinners (15:2), praises the faith of a Gentile (7:9), makes a Samaritan the hero of a parable (10:33), and shows no embarrassment over being seen in public with women (7:37-50; 8:2-3). The reason is obvious: "the Son of Man came to seek out and to save the lost" (Luke 19:10).

In every way, Jesus fulfilled (through his ministry and the subsequent ministry of his church) the Isaiahnic prophecy he had read in his hometown Synagogue at the outset of his ministry:

> The Spirit of the Lord is upon me, because he has anointed me to bring good news to the poor. He has sent me to proclaim release to the captives and recovery of sight to the blind, to let the oppressed go free, to proclaim the year of the Lord's favor. (Luke 4:18-19)

From this proclamation, we are given a glimpse into the kind of savior Luke's Jesus sees himself to be; throughout Luke-Acts, it is clear that the salvation Jesus brings is all encompassing, as Joel Green explains:

> Luke holds together what the contemporary church has often partitioned into discordant elements: empowering the disadvantaged, seeking the lost, reconciling persons across social lines, calling people to repentance, healing the sick, forgiving sins, initiating people into the community of God's people. All of these and more are constitutive of salvation in the Third Gospel. (Green:136)

The early Christians, empowered by the Holy Spirit picked up this ministry and carried the message of universal salvation to virtually the whole world (Acts 2:21; 4:12; 16:17; 28:28, et al.). They shared the good news of salvation with Jew and Gentile (Acts 2:36; 17:22), captive and free (Acts 16:25; 16:31), male and female (16:11-18). In the Acts, there is no place the disciples are not willing to go, and no one that they seem willing to overlook with their message. To be a Christian, then, is to be a part of a saved community that is seeking to share that salvation with the world.

The Christology of John

In John, Jesus is presented as God's divine son (Fuller and Perkins: 96-108). This is demonstrated in a number of ways. First, Jesus' divinity is plainly asserted by John. He is called the Word who was not only "with" God in the beginning, but was himself God —the very Creator (1:1-3; 18). The evangelist reports several miraculous "signs" for the stated purpose of leading people to believe that Jesus is "the Messiah, the Son of God" (John 20:30-31), which is the essence of the confession made by Thomas. When he sees the resurrected body of Jesus with his own eyes, Thomas blurts out: "My Lord and my God" (John 20:28). John's purpose is to lead his readers to make the same confession so that they might "have life in his [Jesus'] name" (John 20:31).

Second, Jesus' divinity is implied in the way that he makes use of a divine name. When Moses encountered the God of his ancestors in the burning bush, he asked by what name he was to identify God. The response was "I AM WHO I AM" (Exodus 3:14). Moses was to tell his people that he was sent by "I AM." Over and again in John, Jesus applies the phase "I am" to himself. This mode of self-identification is an apparent echo of the divine name. Often it is followed by a predicate: "I am the bread of life" (6:35); "I am the light of the world" (8:12); "I am the door" (John 10:9); "I am the good shepherd" (John 10:11). At other times it is used without a predicate: "Jesus said to them, 'Very truly, I tell you, before Abraham was, I am" (John 8:58); "...for you will die in your sins unless you believe that I am he" (John 8:24). According to Fuller and Perkins, "Within the narrative, Jesus' identity with God reaches its fullest expression when he pronounces the divine "I Am" (101).

Third, Jesus' divine sonship is seen in his insistence that God is his father, which was taken to mean that he saw himself as equal with God (5:17-18; 8:58; 10:33; 19:7). John's Jesus is not simply a son of God in the sense that he was created by God (e.g., Adam Luke 3:38), or in the sense that he was a member of the Israelite community (Exodus 4:22; Hosea 11:1), or even in the sense that he was in some way a king (Psalm 2:7). Instead, the narrative pushes its readers to see Jesus as the "only Son of God" (John 1:14,18; 3:16; 18), who was "one" with his father (John 10:30). As God's divine son, "Jesus is given functions preserved elsewhere for God only (e.g., judgment, 8:16, resurrection of the dead, 6:39-40, and bestowal of life, 10:28; 11:25-26)" (Kysar:924). In fact, seeing him was the same as seeing his heavenly Father (14:9).

This emphasis on Jesus' divinity does not result in a denial of his humanity. As Luke Johnson has observed,

> The Jesus in John's Gospel is in some ways even more human than in the Synoptics [the other three Gospels]. He experiences fatigue (4:6) and indecision (7:1-10) and anguish (12:7; 13:21). He is convulsed at the death of his friend Lazarus (11:33-35). He performs a miracle for the pleasure of it (2:1-11) and shows irritation (2:4; 6:26; 7:6-8; 8:25) and suspicion (2:24-25). He asks for a positive response from others (6:66-71). Only in this Gospel is Jesus portrayed as having friends

> (11:1-12:9). He has a disciple he prefers more than others (13:23; 19:26; 20:2; 21:20). (1996:156)

This divine son, then, who is undeniably human, reveals the nature and intentions of God in understandable (human) terms (1:18; 14:9).

John's picture of Jesus might have been especially comforting to a community of followers who were facing rejection by the Jews, persecution by the Romans, and theological corruption from incipient Gnosticism. Unlike the Jews, John's community found that God was revealed most clearly by Jesus (rather than Moses); unlike the Romans, they would worship the Christ (rather than the Emperor); and unlike the Gnostics, they would affirm that Jesus was "the Word [who] became flesh and lived among us" (John 1:14a).

A Summary of Gospel Christologies

This survey has shown that the four Gospels present a range of christological viewpoints. The temptation to choose one over the other must be resisted, as Dupuis observes:

> the distinct New Testament Christologies need to be kept in fruitful tension and dialogue, lest, choosing one at the expense of the other, we should fail to embrace in our vision the fullness of the mystery and perhaps lose sight of either the authentic humanhood of Jesus or of his true divine Sonship. (74)

And, the diversity must not be pressed to the extreme. Luke Johnson argues that though the differences are important, there is a distinct messianic pattern that comes through not only the Gospels, but also the rest of the New Testament books (1996:141-166).

While the four evangelists clearly focus on different aspects of Jesus' identity, they do not present four contradictory christologies. The Matthean emphasis of Jesus' superiority may be found also in Mark (10:29), Luke (11:31-32), and John (6:68). The Markan emphasis on the suffering king is present in Matthew (27:11, 29, 37, 42), Luke (19:38, 23:38), and John (1:49; 18:37; 19:19). Luke's portrayal of Jesus as universal savior is echoed in Matthew (1:21; 18:11), Mark (8:35; 13:13), and John (3:17; 4:42; 5:34; 12:47). John's Christology of divine sonship is at least implied in various synoptic passages (Matthew 11:27; 16:16; Mark 14:36; Luke 1:35). In discussing the same person, the Gospels tell his story in ways that reveal important facets of his identity and met specific needs of the evangelists' differing communities. This must always be the case; for those who will proclaim the story of Jesus must do so from within their own specific contexts and tell it in a language that is meaningful to the listening world (Hilkert:446).

Early Extremes

Before the infant church reached the end of the apostolic age (C.E. 100), problematic positions regarding the nature of Jesus Christ arose. The two most commonly cited errors represent opposite extremes on a continuum. A group of Jewish Christians called Ebionites ("poor ones") contended that Jesus was merely a man (Ignatius, To The Philadelphians:82). They saw Jesus as someone who was special because he had done something no one before him had done —he obeyed the Mosaic law perfectly. By this accomplishment, Jesus was named the Christ of God. The Ebionites sought to imitate Jesus in his observance of the Mosaic law and believed that they too could achieve the status of Christ by fulfilling the law themselves (Hyppolytus:114). Apparently their strict Jewish monotheism hindered them from attributing divinity to Jesus.

The Docetics, in stark contrast, believed Jesus was a totally divine being who only "seemed" (Greek dokeo —"I seem") to be a man. The human history of Jesus was only an act; for as deity, he was incapable of genuine suffering or death. This view grew out of a dualistic philosophy that judged the material world to be evil and the spiritual realm holy; integration of the two was thought to be impossible. So, since Jesus was divine, he could not have been a physical man (possessing a material body).

The presence of at least incipient forms of these extremes in the apostolic Church is obvious from the fact that they are challenged in the New Testament. The Gospel of John intentionally contradicts both views, arguing that Jesus was not only God and the eternally-existing Word (John 1:1-3), but that that same Word "became flesh and lived among us" in the person of Jesus Christ (John 1:14). The epistle of 1 John adds that the Word's cohabitation with humanity was not merely apparent, but was seen with human eyes and felt with human hands. To deny that Christ had actually come in the flesh was heresy (1 John 1:1; 4:1-3).

Controversy, Councils, and Confessions

These views (as well as many that fell in between) were vigorously opposed by Christian writers who saw in them the denial of apostolic teaching (see Hyppolytus, Irenaeus, et. al). Although rejected as heresies, these views did not die completely. Nor did their rejection result in complete unanimity of opinion about the identity of Jesus. Confusion over how Jesus could be truly God and truly human at the same time persisted (O'Collins:153-201; Macquarrie:147-172). So tenacious was this confusion that it was the focus of several Ecumenical Councils; two are especially noteworthy. The Council of Nicea convened to address the teaching of Arius, priest of Alexandria, who argued that though Jesus was divine and like God, he was inferior to God. In C.E. 325 under the leadership of Athanasius, bishop of Alexandria, the council issued its creed:

> We believe in one God, the Father Almighty, maker of all things visible and invisible; and in one Lord Jesus Christ, the Son of God, the only-begotten of his Father, of the substance of the Father, God of God, Light of Light, very God of very God, begotten, not made, being of one substance with the Father. By whom all things were made, both which be in heaven and in earth. Who for us men and for our salvation came down [from heaven] and was incarnate and was made man. He suffered and the third day he rose again, and ascended to heaven. And he shall come again to judge both the quick and the dead....(Percival:3)

So, it was the council's conviction that Jesus was both "very God," and "made man." But, how can the same person be both God and man? Nicea had not adequately answered this. It remained to be addressed a century-and-a-quarter later by the Council of Chalcedon.

The 150 council members met to respond to the teaching of Eutychus, a church leader from Constantinople, who argued that Jesus had only one nature: his divine nature had in some way dissolved his human nature. The Council rejected Eutychus' view and declared that Jesus was one person with two natures:

> ...we teach with one voice that the Son [of God] and our Lord Jesus Christ is to be confessed as one and the same [Person], that he is perfect in Godhead and perfect in manhood, very God and very man, of a reasonable soul and [human] body consisting, consubstantial with the Father as touching his Godhead, and consubstantial with us as touching his manhood.... This one and the same Jesus Christ, the only-begotten Son [of God] must be confessed in two natures, unconfusedly, immutably, indivisibly, inseparably [united], and that without the distinction of natures being taken away by such union....(Percival:264-265)

It is significant to note that the council chose to clarify the meaning of the two natures in negative terms. In a sense, they, "put up four fences (without confusion, without change, without division, without separation) and said: 'The mystery lies within this area'" (Runia:12-13). Although this confession did not really answer the question as to how Jesus could have both natures at the same time, it respected both aspects of the New Testament's teaching about Jesus' identity and stood as the fundamental statement of Christology for many centuries. This is not to say Chalcedon was universally accepted, as the existence of the Nestorian, Armenian,

Coptic, and Jacobite Churches (to mention a few), demonstrates. This confession has, however, stood as the dominant christological benchmark for Catholic and Protestant Christianity.

Renaissance, Reformation, and Enlightenment

In the years since Chalcedon, three major intellectual movements have occurred: the Renaissance, the Reformation, and the Enlightenment. Each of these movements exerted important influences on christological studies. The Renaissance (beginning in 1453 with the fall of Constantinople) was an age of increased interest in learning and of the study of ancient literature. The established standards of thought in learning and the arts were challenged and the Church began to lose its privileged voice in these areas. The Renaissance attitude is often expressed in the humanistic phrase: "Man [sic.] is the measure of all things." This increased interest in the study of ancient literature opened the door for scholars to begin to appreciate the intellectual and literary context in which the Gospel story arose.

The Reformation (beginning in 1517 when Martin Luther nailed his list of theological grievances with Rome on the church door in Wittenberg, Germany) fostered an attitude that was suspicious of religious dogma. A dominant theme of this period was an emphasis on the "priesthood of all believers." In its wake, people would require more than papal directives and official creeds as the basis for belief in specific doctrines.

The Enlightenment (beginning in 1642 with the publication of René Descartes' Meditations II) marked an intentional turn toward the priority of reason over superstition and Church authority. The coronation of reason as king represents the Enlightenment disposition and encouraged antagonism against Christianity's claims on history. Dominant among the voices that characterized the period were those belonging to: René Descartes (1596-1650) who taught the world that doubt is a virtue; David Hume (1711-1776) who contended that miracles are impossible; and Immanuel Kant (1724-1804) who challenged humans to think for themselves, even in matters of religion —to "dare to know" (Kant:132-139). This age of Enlightenment (ca. 1642-1800) and the subsequent Modern period (ca. 1800-1960), so characterized by rationalism, enabled deism and full-blown skepticism to gain respectability. As a result, Chalcedon's confession came under fire.

Beginning with Hermann S. Reimarus (1694-1768), scholars began to suggest that the "historical Jesus" was a very different person from the "Christ of faith" described in the Gospels (and the classical creeds). Reimarus[5] made a "sharp distinction between the intention of Jesus during his life and the intention of his disciples after his death" (Borg:42).

Reimarus believed that Jesus' intentions (rebellion against Rome) were thwarted by his death and that the disciples invented the resurrection story and deified their Teacher as a way of keeping his movement alive. New Testament scholarship of the last 200 years has largely adopted as paradigmatic this distinction between the historical Jesus (the Jesus who emerges when the Gospels are subjected to the rigors of the historical-critical method) and the Christ of Christian faith (the version/s of Jesus presented by the New Testament writers and the confessions of Christendom).

Three Quests for the Historical Jesus

The "Old Quest"

This paradigm spawned three "Quests" for the historical Jesus (following summary based on Wright:1-18 and Strimple).[6] The first (Old) Quest, which began with the writings of Hermann S. Reimarus and terminated with Albert Schweitzer's classic Quest of the Historical Jesus (published in 1906), sought to discover what —if anything —could be known of the historical Jesus. Scholars working in this period rejected the idea that Jesus was the miracle-working God-incarnate who intentionally founded the Christian faith. Instead, they saw rationalistic explanations for the miracles and credited Jesus' followers with creating Christianity (either out of intentional fraud or out of superstitious ignorance). Early Old Questers saw Jesus as an eschatological prophet who failed; later Old Questers saw him primarily as a good moral teacher of ethical truths. To the former, the New Testament documents tell us a great deal about the early church, but virtually nothing about Jesus. Their writings were primarily critiques of the Gospels. To the latter, Jesus is important to the Christian Faith in so much as he embodied and revealed God's love. They had no need for a literal incarnation or resurrection. According to them, we can affirm the Easter faith without the Easter message when we love as Jesus taught. Their writings often took the form of romantic portrayals of the life Jesus-—embellished to look and think like a liberal-minded humanitarian.

In 1906 Albert Schweitzer surveyed the work of scholars from H.S. Reimarus to William Wrede (1859-1906) and concluded that after almost a century and a half, they had gotten no closer to their goal. Schweitzer asserted that those who preceded him had succeeded only in finding the kind of Jesus they set out to find: the deists had found a deistic Jesus; the liberals had found a loving teacher of timeless ethical truths. The historical Jesus Schweitzer found was a repulsive apocalyptic prophet-figure whose teaching has very little value for us today. Schweitzer's judgment on the futility of the Quest was so authoritative that the enterprise was abandoned for almost forty years.

In the wake of Schweitzer, Karl Barth and Rudolph Bultmann dominated the scene of Christian theology. They neither believed the historical Jesus could be discovered, nor did they have a need for such a discovery. Barth was comfortable with the classical creeds; what mattered to him was the Christ of faith. For Bultmann, although he admitted that in theory there was an historical core behind the New Testament mythology (e.g., such things as Jesus' miracles and resurrection), what really mattered was the believer's personal encounter with God through the biblical story. In his way of thinking, the resurrection of Jesus, for example, was not about a man being raised from the dead, but about the believer's freedom to live in the world as though he or she was not of the world.

The "New Quest"

The second (New) Quest, begun by Ernst Käsemann in 1953, has sought to determine what the historical Jesus actually said, and to ponder what those "authentic" words might reveal about him. Käsemann, a student of Bultmann, disagreed with his mentor over the value of the historical Jesus to faith. While he agreed that a "life of Jesus" (i.e., a biography of Jesus such as those attempted in the preceding century) could not be written, he believed that in order for Jesus to be the foundation of Christian faith, something of him must be knowable. New Questers have thus sought to discover, by isolating his authentic words, how Jesus understood himself. The upshot of this interest in the words of Jesus was a sustained critical interest in the parables (thought by some to be more nearly authentic than the longer discourses attributed to Jesus) as well as a deeper reflection upon the way the evangelists set out to compose their narratives.

Although New Questers, such as C.H. Dodd, Gunther Bornkamm, Joachim Jeremias, Edward Schillebeeckx have contributed significantly to contemporary understandings of the Gospels and have contemplated how Jesus might have understood himself, they haven't been very good at bridging the gap from the historical Jesus to the Christ of faith.

This deficiency is especially evident in the work of the Jesus Seminar. In 1985, thirty critical scholars formed an alliance known as the Jesus Seminar. Their purpose was to carry on the Quest for the historical Jesus and to disseminate their findings far beyond the cloistered halls of academia. Since its inception, the number of fellows has increased to over 200. The group isolated approximately 500 sayings traditionally attributed to Jesus and put each one to a vote to determine its level of authenticity. After all the votes were cast, the fellows of the Seminar published their results in the form of a book, The Five Gospels: The Search for the

Authentic Words of Jesus (Macmillan: 1993). This volume contains a brief summary of the scholars' philosophy and agenda, their color-coded translation of Mark, Matthew, Luke, John, and the Gospel of Thomas (called the Scholar's Version) and a commentary-like discussion of all passages containing words attributed to Jesus. All the words they were confident Jesus actually spoke were printed in red; all words they felt Jesus probably spoke were printed in pink. The sayings that were considered less genuine were printed in gray (signifying that although the words aren't Jesus' the thoughts are similar to his) and bold black (reserved for words the fellows were certain neither originated with Jesus nor reflected his ideas). In the final analysis, these scholars determined that only about 18% of what is normally attributed to Jesus is authentic; the rest was put into his mouth by the evangelists.[7]

The picture of Jesus that emerged from this research was that of a witty vagabond who traveled about begging bread and issuing social commentary (Funk:1-38). Cynic sages from first century Rome —such as Diogenes of Sinope —provided the model for this new portrait of Jesus. Seminar sympathizer, Burton Mack, described the sage in this way: "The public image was that of a lone beggar who had renounced the comforts of life to pit himself against the elements and practice the virtues of living with little" (Mack:115). The "Cynic's purpose was to point out the disparities sustained by the social system and refuse to let the system put him in his place" (116).

According to John Dominic Crossan (co-chair of the group), "Jesus was a peasant Jewish Cynic" and his first followers were "hippies in a world of Augustan yuppies" (Crossan, 1994:198). This cynic was no more a child of God than anyone else, was not born of a virgin and performed no miracles. He angered the wrong people, and for that was executed like a criminal. His dead body was likely dug from its shallow grave and devoured by wild dogs (Crossan as quoted by Russell Watson, "A Lesser Child of God," Newsweek, April 4, 1994; and Richard N. Ostling, "Jesus Christ, Plain and Simple" Time, January 10, 1994).

When the Seminar's "laconic sage" is carefully examined, though, it is difficult to understand why Jewish or Roman authorities would have felt threatened enough by him to put him to death (Hays:43-48). What is even harder to imagine is how this particular Jesus of history could have become the Christ of faith. It stretches the limits of credulity to believe the Fellows' cynic sage was able to inspire a movement that has proved as virulent as Christianity.

The "Third Quest"

The Third Quest, overlapping chronologically with the New Quest, is an effort by contemporary scholars to determine what may be known of the historical Jesus within the rich context of first century Judaism. E.P. Sanders is a highly respected representative of this group.[8] His is a calm and reserved voice in a discipline that is often characterized by extremists. Sanders argues that, from a historian's perspective, a great deal about Jesus may be known. He summarizes what he believes to be the facts about the historical Jesus that are almost beyond dispute:

> Jesus was born c. 4 BCE, near the time of the death of Herod the Great;
>
> he spent his childhood and early adult years in Nazareth, a Galilean village;
>
> he was baptized by John the Baptist;
>
> he called disciples;
>
> he taught in the towns, villages and countryside of Galilee (apparently not the cities);
>
> he preached 'the kingdom of God';
>
> about the year 30 he went to Jerusalem for Passover;
>
> he created a disturbance in the Temple area;
>
> he had a final meal with the disciples;
>
> he was arrested and interrogated by Jewish authorities, specifically the high priest;
>
> he was executed on the orders of the Roman prefect, Pontius Pilate. (10-11)

Closely related to this outline of Jesus' life, Sanders adds these "equally sure facts about the aftermath of Jesus' life":

> his disciples at first fled;
>
> they saw him (in what sense is not certain) after his death;
>
> as a consequence, they believed that he would return to found the kingdom;
>
> they formed a community to await his return and sought to win others to faith in him as God's Messiah. (11)

Sanders elaborated on this outline by bringing his knowledge of first century Judaism into conversation with a critically-sensitive understanding of the canonical gospels. He believes Jesus was a religious teacher who was convinced that he spoke for God and that his followers would have a place in God's coming kingdom (238). He was not so much a reformer, as he was a representative ("viceroy") of God who demonstrated God's acceptance of people in ways that contradicted the normal religious standards. Had Jesus called sinners to repentance, his work would have been praised, not renounced by the religious leaders of his day. Although he saw himself as having an especially intimate relationship with God, he probably did not see himself as the Messiah (242-243).

When Jesus arrived in Jerusalem for Passover, he did so during a time when the rulers would be fearful of civil unrest. In this charged climate, he sealed his fate by speaking and acting in ways that were critical of the temple and the socio-religious system it represented (249-275). The rulers had to keep peace, and Jesus threatened that peace. Pilate callously sent Jesus to the cross for the same reason (273-275).

Although Sanders admits that he does not know what to make of the disciples' resurrection experiences, he does not doubt that they experienced something. It was their conviction that he was raised that empowered them to go forth and change human history.

Admittedly, there is much good to be found in the writings of Third Quest scholars. However, they still fail to provide an adequate bridge to carry one from the Jesus of history to the Christ of faith. Even if they can construct a plausible scenario whereby Jesus' original followers came to believe he was worthy of praise and worship, they come short of showing how contemporary disciples can justify faith in Jesus as Savior.

Other Approaches

As important as the "historical-Jesus-versus-the-Christ-of-faith" paradigm has been, it is by no means the only way to approach Christology. Eighteen hundred years of christological reflection preceded it and even in the years since Reimarus many thinkers have traveled other roads in the pursuit to understand the identity of this man from Galilee. As far back as 1892, Martin Kähler reprimanded those preoccupied with historical Jesus studies. Such efforts were as odious to him as were the classical creeds they were intended to supplant. Kähler instead contended that the real Christ was neither the Christ of the creeds nor the Christ who was being portrayed by the Old Questers. The "real Christ is the Christ who is preached" (66). In other words, since the Gospels are biased documents written by people who already believed in Christ, they cannot be mined for historical information (in the modern sense) that when assembled will give us a more accurate picture of the real Jesus. The only "real" Jesus available to us is the very one we meet in the Scriptures.

Christology from Above or Below

There is another paradigm some have found useful in exploring the identity of Jesus. It has to do with the direction one moves in understanding the relationship between the two natures (to use Chalcedonian language) of Jesus. One may either begin from "above" or from "below." For example, one may approach Jesus from his humanity (below) that we first encounter in the Gospels (as the baby in the manger, the child circumcised in the temple, the lost and found adolescent, etc.) and then proceed to the issues of preexistence and heavenly exaltation (that we encounter in the Johannine prologue and the christological hymns in the Pauline corpus). Or, one may approach Jesus from his deity (above) as the second person of the trinity and then proceed to the issues of his becoming human (in the incarnation) and his life, ministry, and death.[9]

Whereas Christians typically assume that moving from "above" to "below" is the correct order (because it is, in a sense, the chronological order), this approach has often proved detrimental to Christian faith. This is so because when one begins with a divine Jesus, one has difficulty seeing the human side of the Lord as any more than an act (God acting like a human). Consequently, before one honestly struggles with the human limitations of the man born in Bethlehem (such as his need to learn, feel pain, wonder about the future, etc.), one has already dismissed them as affectations. Operating "from above" tends to encourage doceticism; Jesus' full humanity is often sacrificed.

This is not to say that moving from below to above is entirely risk-free. One can get so caught up in the humanity of Jesus that it becomes impossible for one to accept the New Testament's insistence that he was "in the beginning with God" (John 1:2; John 17:5; Philippians 2:6-11, et al.). One can fall into ebionitism; Jesus' true deity can be sacrificed.

Interestingly, though, the New Testament favors moving from below to above (Fuller and Perkins:5-8). This is the order that the disciples first encountered Jesus, and it is the direction that the Synoptics tell their stories. In Matthew and Luke, specifically, we meet a baby, who grows to manhood, and eventually ascends to the heavenly realm. Peter described Jesus in the first Christian sermon as: "Jesus of Nazareth, a man attested to you by God" (2:22). Paul described Jesus as the "last Adam" (1 Corinthians 15:45), and said that God's "son" was "born of a woman" (Galatians 4:4). It is probably not accidental that the "from above" prologue of John was among the last canonical documents penned. Since both "above" and "below" material is found in Scripture, it is important to respect both, and to avoid emphasizing one at the expense of the other (O'Collins:16-17).[10]

This distinction is, however, according to Moltmann, "both superficial and misleading because to know Jesus Christ practically and specifically can only be a matter of dialectical conditions. . . we have to look at Jesus' humanity in order to know his divinity, and we have to contemplate his divinity so as to know his humanity." He thus concludes:

> Anyone who resolves this dialectical process of perception into dogmatic alternatives, is resolving —or dissolving —Christology altogether. That person will end up with a theological Christology without Jesus, or with an anthropological Jesusology without God. It is therefore high time that we abandoned the infelicitous phraseology 'from above' and 'from below' in Christology, in order to turn to the more complex processes of coming to know Jesus Christ. (69)

Functional Versus Ontological Christology

A similar distinction is sometimes made between what are termed "functional" and "ontological" christologies. This is the difference between approaching Christology primarily in terms of Jesus' work on our behalf or in terms of his essential nature. Whereas the classical creeds come to us in strongly ontological language (i.e., language that describes the "nature" or "essence" of things), the New Testament spends more time discussing Jesus' functions as our prophet, priest, and king (in short, as the Messiah). This is largely a theoretical distinction, however, because as O'Collins points out, "to reflect on the activity of Christ, while denying all knowledge of his being, would be to attempt the impossible." After all, he says, "function follows being" (20).

Postmodern Christology

As the third Christian millennium dawns, many scholars contend that the Western world is in the throes of a new intellectual era. For them, history can be divided into three periods: pre-modern (also referred to as "pre-critical"), modern, and postmodern. The fulcrum upon which this scheme pivots is modernism with its emphasis on rationalism and empirical science. At the risk of oversimplification, the three periods may be conceived in the following way. The pre-modern world was theologically oriented: "Repeatedly and sporadically-—but supremely in Jesus Christ—-God entered the realm of human affairs from a lofty position above the world. . ." (Grenz:61). God was at the apex and humans were "a little lower than the angels" (Psalm 8:5, KJV).

With the advent of the modern world, skepticism (with its bias against the supernatural) replaced God's activities with natural laws. The "miraculous" became a problematic category and a view of history developed that methodologically excluded miracles. Accordingly, modern people could no longer speak of miracles as historical because they lack present-day analogy (i.e., they aren't happening now) and they do not fit into a chain of naturalistic causes and effects (they are, of course, "supernatural"). These two criteria, articulated by Ernst Troeltsch in his 1898 essay Historical and Dogmatic Method in Theology (13-14), have typified the modern method of approaching history and defined the limits of such research for almost a century. Modern scholars, freed from the miraculous, searched for a "historical" Jesus who lacked supernatural power. They constructed christologies that were more anthropological than theological.

Jürgen Moltmann observes that just as the pre-critical period's preoccupation with metaphysical Christology gave way to the modern period's fascination with questions of the historical Jesus, so now, as the curtain falls on the modern world, the spotlight is shifting to the distinctly postmodern concerns of ecology and cosmology (xvi). This is not to say that metaphysical and historical concerns cease to matter in postmodernity, only that they are no longer primary. Postmodern Christology of the kind developed by Moltmann recasts each of these foci within wider horizons and translates them into new situations. So, his Christology locates the nature and history of Jesus within a cosmological landscape. It is informed, but not enslaved, by the previous paradigms.

Moltmann calls for "Christology in messianic dimensions." That is, he sees Jesus Christ to be the complete fulfillment of the messianic hope of the Old Testament prophets. But his is not simply the Jewish Jesus of the Third Quest, for he holds resolutely onto the uniqueness of the Trinitarian perspective of Christianity (xvi-xvii). By re-visiting the messianic expectation, he re-captures the vision of God's messiah destined to redeem not only humanity, but the entire cosmos.

His starting point echoes Bonhoeffer's question, "Who is Jesus Christ for us today?" But Moltmann wishes to ask the question specifically in light of the new reality created for humanity by the atomic bomb and the naming of the third world. No longer is mortality a concern only of human individuals; but since Hiroshima, the entire human race and the Earth as well must face mortality (46). Moltmann attempts to take in the broadest possible view of humanity's plight—including political, economic, social, and ecological forces of oppression and danger —and to show that Jesus the Messiah and the kingdom he brings is the answer to it all.

This "messianic Christology" is explained under five rubrics: (1) The messianic mission of Jesus —as God's prophet of the poor, Jesus showed in his earthly ministry the priorities and ethical concerns of God for humanity (73-150). (2) The apocalyptic passion of Jesus —in his suffering and death, Jesus completely empathizes with all suffering and death in the cosmos. On the cross, deity also experiences death (151-212). (3) The eschatological resurrection of Christ —in his resurrection, Jesus "acts as the embodied promise for the whole creation" (258, 213-273). Jesus' resurrection began a process that will eventually sweep all of creation. (4) The cosmic Christ —Christ is to be seen in his three-fold capacity: the creator, the moving power of evolution, and the redeemer of the entire cosmos (274-312). (5) The parousia of Christ —Christ's coming brings the consummation of the messianic purposes of God —when all will finally be made right with God (313-341).

What makes Moltmann's approach especially appealing is that it takes both the biblical text and the contemporary world seriously and attempts to avoid one-sided solutions to the major christological controversies. It sees the intentions of God for humanity and the rest of the created realm as a living reality in the person of Jesus of Nazareth. It envisions the time when all that is broken will be mended and when all oppression will cease (a process that has begun in the actions of those led by the Spirit, and will be finally and completely fulfilled in the kingdom of God (98-103)). It sees in the death of Jesus on the cross the coming end of all death and suffering in this world, and sees in Jesus' resurrection the foreshadowing of the new era where death no longer has a hold on the cosmos.

This is a Christology that is filled with ethical implications as well. Under each rubric, Moltmann shows how in practical terms the community that is created by the Gospel participates in the messianic mission of Jesus. His Christology necessarily results in christopraxis:

> It is a way of life, a way in which people learn who Jesus is, learn it with all their senses, acting and suffering, in work and prayer. To know Jesus does not simply mean learning facts of christological dogma. It means learning to know him in the praxis of discipleship. (43)

Summary and Trajectory

Paul wrote, "To me, living is Christ and dying is gain" (Philippians 1:21). For this early follower of Jesus, a total change had occurred in his life. He who once believed Christians did not deserve to live, came to believe being a Christian was the only reason to live. There was no question in Paul's mind that his identity had been completely reshaped by his encounter with, and his continual relationship with, Jesus Christ. Paul's experience is presented in the New Testament as paradigmatic for subsequent generations. He even called upon fellow Christians to follow his example (1 Corinthians 11:1).

So, Christology is fundamental to Christianity, and it is intended to be identity-shaping. It is not enough to give mental chase to the great christological conundrums that have occupied theologians and academics for two millennia. It is not even enough to simply mouth the words of the orthodox Christian confessions. Both of these can occur without a substantive change in either the individual or the world. What the New Testament Scriptures call us to see, however, is that Jesus changes everything. Christian conversion is about that change occurring on an individual level and the Christian church is about that change being lived out in community.

This chapter has briefly surveyed the way the Church has struggled through the years to understand the identity of Jesus Christ. Each effort at understanding has implications for the shaping of Christian identity. The earliest communities —especially those represented by the evangelists — expressed their understanding of the identity of Jesus in diverse, yet broadly similar terms. From their writings we can recognize what Luke Johnson calls a "pattern":

> ...the four canonical Gospels are remarkably consistent on one essential aspect of the identity and mission of Jesus. Their fundamental focus is not on Jesus' wondrous deeds nor on his wise words. Their shared focus is upon the character of his life and death. They all reveal the same pattern of radical obedience to God and selfless love toward other people. (1996:157-158)

This "pattern" is the christological foundation for much of what is said in the epistles and is recognizable in the lives described in the book of Acts. It is the conviction of Johnson, as well as the central premise of this project that the Gospel story has an identity-shaping function for those who follow Jesus:

> All four Gospels also agree that discipleship is to follow the same messianic pattern. They do not emphasize the performance of certain deeds or the learning of certain doctrines. They insist on living according to the same pattern of life and death shown by Jesus. (1996:158)

Unfortunately, the history of Christology is rife with attempts to shape the identity of Jesus according to prevailing philosophies. This tendency is easily seen in the Ebionite and Docetic heresies: the former fashioned a Jesus who fit more appropriately into their rigid monotheism, and the latter fashioned a Jesus who fit more appropriately into their dualism. But this problem is also at the root of much modern Christology. The three "Quests" have and continue to consistently turn up Jesuses that resemble the preconceived notions of those who've gone searching. The challenge of Christianity, though, is to meet the true Jesus of Scripture, and to be reshaped by that encounter. This will mean, meeting in the Gospels the "singular, unsubstitutable person" of Jesus of Nazareth (Frei, 1975:52), and not the person we wish him to be (such as someone like us), nor a mere literary pattern for us to imitate (that is, a "Christ figure").

Because this "singular, unsubstitutable person" of Jesus of Nazareth is met primarily in the Gospel narratives, the next chapter explores narrative as genre and considers how the narrative works in mediating an encounter between Jesus and contemporary women and men. It is this encounter, and its impact on the lives of Jesus' followers that is the focus of this project.

CHAPTER 3

NARRATIVE AND CHRISTIAN IDENTITY

Introduction

Like Bob (whose plight was described in chapter one), many members of the Church of Christ can identify with —and feel the indictment of —the following words:

> Ask the average church member to describe the difference between himself as he would be without God, and himself as he is with God. He will be hard put to give an intelligent answer. The difference between godless John Doe and godly John Doe (on John's showing) is so slight that you wonder, and so does he, why we should send off missionaries thousands of miles to induce others to enjoy these microscopic changes. (Foreman:135)

This is an apt description of the painful frustration caused by our identity crisis. I believe that part of the blame for this present reality may be laid at the feet of the Enlightenment. As a particularly modern expression of Christianity, the Church of Christ was birthed in the delivery room of New World democracy and midwifed by reformers schooled in common sense realism.[11]

As Old World churches battled one another for dominance in a fledgling nation of people intoxicated on the new wine of democratic freedom, the reformers preached a message of unity based on doctrinal agreement. By laying aside human creeds, all believers could be united on the Bible alone, the reformers assured the world. The unity they sought turned out to be much more elusive than they ever could have imagined. By making agreement upon a set of doctrinal distinctives the pathway to unity, they spawned a movement that has been more polemical than ecumenical.[12]

A Narrative Vantage Point

One of the negative legacies of the Enlightenment is the prioritizing of logic over art and propositions over narratives. So with the development of modern history, the power of story was undermined (thus, the charge: "That is just a story, but this is history"). Story came to be thought of as fiction (and, in the minds of many, untrue), and history gained the status of "truth" (it was, after all, what really happened). This distinction, however, belied the embarrassing and irritating reality that histories are colored by many things and that the line between historical "fact" and fiction is often the private and carefully guarded possession of the historian. So, histories are continually rewritten.

What got lost in all this, was an appreciation for the power of story and the fact that so much of our conceptual world is story. We are, after all, beings who live —and relive —life in narrative form.[13] We understand and define ourselves by the stories of which we are a part and that we tell. This may be demonstrated by recalling something as simple as introducing a friend to another person. One might begin by naming the friend's good qualities (he or she is smart, loving, kind, gentle, dependable, etc.), but before long is likely say something like, "for example..." or "Let me tell you about this one time when she or he did...". Or consider the act of introducing a distinguished scholar to an assembly of colleagues. While the audience might hear a simple recitation of the scholar's educational degrees and awards (an admittedly non-narrative form of discourse), the introduction is only meaningful to those who understand the typical story that accompanies those credentials. It is the audience's awareness of that implied story that makes the introduction effective. The sense that one really "knows" another person rarely precedes a shared experience with him or her. That experience comes in the form of, and is retold as, a story. So, to really identify a person one tells a story.

The same is true for the way one identifies oneself. How many of us have heard ourselves self-consciously confess to a new acquaintance, "Well, I didn't mean to tell you my whole life's story"? And yet, it is precisely in the telling of our stories that we reveal who we are and allow others the opportunity to get to know us.[14]

Fortunately, the modernistic mindset has been weighed in the balance and found wanting.[15] The past few decades truly have been a period of renaissance for story. Modernity's false dichotomies are giving way to a more balanced understanding that art can speak the truth just as well as logic, and often does so more effectively.[16] The days of merely mining the stories of the Bible for the hidden ore of propositional truth from which the shiny metals of systematic theology could be refined is finally passing away and we are beginning to have ears to (once again) hear the Bible's stories as stories that impact our lives in transformational ways. Perhaps we are now better able to understand the apostle Paul's assertion that the Gospel story is the "power of God for the salvation of everyone who believes" (Romans 1:16). If so, then maybe an echo of Paul's voice may be heard in George Lindbeck's thesis that Christians are people "who have learned the stories of Israel, Jesus, and the Church well enough that now they interpret their own lives and the world itself in terms of those stories" (Barnes:50).[17]

A Personal Epiphany

"Woe to me!" I cried. "I am ruined! For I am a person of rationalistic mind and I live among a people of rationalistic minds, and my eyes have seen the King, the Lord of Story." Like the ancient prophet, my world changed when I saw God from a new vantage point. Isaiah's change came in reaction to a visual picture that unfolded before his entranced eyes (Isaiah 6:1-4). My change came in reaction to mental images of the Gospel that were painted by story-weaver's art. When I encountered narrative preaching for the first time it frightened me; it threatened the security my Enlightenment mentality had seemed to provide. Before that day, God existed at a safer distance, and was described with sterile propositions about omniscience, omnipotence and omnibenevolence. My sermons were didactic recitations of biblical facts and Christianity was a philosophy that could be defined and defended with syllogistic discourse. Evangelism was a war comprised of rhetorical battles; to win an argument was to save a soul. This wasn't about emotion, only intellect. Narrative preaching, though, made me vulnerable to "feel" the Gospel (to be touched emotionally, as well as stimulated intellectually).[18] By it I found my heretofore-rationalistic world subverted before I had time to raise my defenses.

At the point when I experienced vulnerability to the Gospel, I met the Lord of Story. Finally, I was given ears to hear the Gospel as story and not as a chain of propositions that had the unfortunate fate of being wrapped in the messy trappings of narration. Only then did it become possible for me to see God as, for example, a woman with broom in hand sweeping the entire universe in search of me —a lost coin (Luke 15:3-10). It became possible for me to hear Luke tell his story of Jesus without jumping to Paul for clarification or to John for supplementation.

I had lived long enough within the artificial world that had been constructed by builders from the Age of Reason. As their structure topples, the reality that we are story beings living in a story world and guided by the stories of Scripture has begun to dawn.[19] While I do not affirm that "there is only story" (Crossan, 1988:29), I do gratefully acknowledge the ubiquitous nature of story. This acknowledgment has practical implications not only about how to read Scripture, but more importantly, about how Christian identity should be shaped.[20]

Identity and Identification

This project's thesis concerns the issue of shaping (and reshaping) Christian identity. In other words, a Christian has a particular personal identity as a Christian that differs from his or her identity before conversion. What is personal identity? Simply put, "Personal identity is an interpretation of personal history" (Stroup:118). It is how a person understands who he or she is. It is the ever-updateable understanding one has of oneself constructed within the context of one's unfolding life story. Put another way,

> Identity is not a substratum, an abstract quintessence situated beyond tensions and crises. On the contrary, as a constant process of identification, it is constituted as concrete identity within the fabric of the adventures and varied fortunes of personal life history. (Bühler:21)

Although quite old, Kenneth Foreman's discussion of the different types of identification is helpful in understanding some of the complexities involved in shaping identity. He suggests that there are as many as five different types of identification:

Type 1: Person A identifies person B with person C. In this case, person A does not know person B, so he or she places person B in the same category as a person C (a person A already knows). Person A may view person C either in a positive or negative light, so in the end, person B is viewed in the same way as person C, be it good or ill. Of course, racial prejudice falls into this category.

Type 2: Person A identifies him/herself with person B. In this case, person A abnegates his/her identity in favor of another person's (e.g., negatively, an insane person may think himself to be God; or positively, a person might classify herself as a part of her church).

Type 3: Person A identifies person B with him/herself. For example, a possessive father might see his son as a mere extension of himself. One person might reach out to another with compassion because she feels the other's pain as if it were her own.

Type 4: Person A thinks he or she is person B and then discovers he or she is actually A and accepts it. This type of identification is useful in paving the way for conversion (e.g., an unregenerate man (A) might believe he is a righteous person (B); it is not until he discovers that he is unregenerate that he is ready to pursue God's plan for regeneration).

Type 5: Person A knows he or she is person A and either rejoices or regrets it. This type of identification is the result of one introspectively evaluating one's identity (as, for example, a Euro-American male), and either regretting or else rejoicing in what one is.

This cursory overview of the types of identification shows clearly that identification is a hermeneutical task; that is, it is an act of interpretation. The goal of this interpretive task is, typically, to produce a coherent, describable identity.

Narrative and Identity

Each of us is living out a personal history created by a mysterious interplay of (at least) genetic predisposition, cultural influence, and personal education and experience. It is a story that actually begins before we are born. Crites suggests, "People awaken to consciousness in a society, with the inner story of experience. . . already infused in cultural forms" (79-80). He explains:

> The stories people hear and tell, the dramas they see performed. . . shape in the most profound way the inner story of experience. We imbibe a sense of the meaning of our own baffling dramas from these stories, and this sense of its meaning in turn affects the form of a man's [sic.] experience and the style of his actions. (79)

Our personal histories provide the raw data out of which our identity stories are hermeneutically crafted. There is more. Our identities are both the interpretation of our stories, as well as the interpretative framework for them. In other words, our identities not only grow out of our stories but they, in turn, shape the way we tell our stories (as we decide what parts of our histories are significant and what parts are incidental, or even too undesirable to repeat). Although we play a significant role in shaping our identities, this act of interpretation is not unique to us; others also busy themselves with the task of interpreting our stories and assigning identity descriptions to us. In turn, their interpretations feed back into our interpretive enterprise (as we either accept or reject their evaluations). The point of all this, however, is that "story" is the "stuff" of our identities as individuals. Hence, one has a "narrative identity, an identity in which man [sic.] can, within the unity of a story, describe himself in the events, the experiences, the tragedies, the joys and the sorrows of his life" (Bühler:21).

As we live, our stories expand and our identities are updated and reinterpreted to take into account the influence of external forces and new experiences. So that, for example, at five, a boy might be identified as "that poor, abandoned orphan." At eight the same boy, now adopted into a wealthy home, might be identified as "that spoiled, rich kid." Yet again, at seventeen he might be identified as "that useless pot-head." Over the same span of years, the child's own interpretation of his identity might evolve from "I'm a bad kid that no one wants" to "I'm a lucky kid to be adopted into such a nice family" to "I am a misunderstood kid who doesn't belong in this place." After reaching adulthood, he might thus interpret his story: "I had a troubled and uncertain childhood, which caused me to feel emotional alienation as an adolescent. Now, I can see how that those experiences have given me a sense of compassion for underprivileged children. That is why I am presently a social worker."

Conversion and Narrative

This interpretive process is at work in what Christians call "conversion" or the "new birth." They understood and described themselves in particular ways (their identities) before they encountered the Gospel and acted in ways that were more or less consistent with such an understanding. But, after encountering the story of Jesus Christ through various means (friends, evangelists, sermons, Scripture), their self-understanding (personal identity) came into question and their personal history had to be "reworked, reinterpreted, and reappropriated" (Stroup:116). Along with this new understanding comes (by implication) a new way of acting. Perhaps the old hymn says it best: "I once was lost, but now I'm found, was blind, but now I see."[21] Ideally, according to Foreman, Christian conversion entails a "threefold identification."

> First I accept the self-identification of Christ with man [sic.] —including me —with all that it entails. I take him as one who has so identified himself with me, with all enmeshed humanity, that he is in very truth our substitute, both in his obedience and in his sacrifice. I accept this in humility and joy. But I accept also this other identification which our Lord willed: that is our becoming one with him. Not for nothing does Paul speak of being crucified with Christ, dying with him, being buried with him. Each of us becomes like Barabbas of the legend, released for some reason he did not understand, stumbling out into empty streets, wandering till he comes upon the crosses whereon hang two of his friends and one man he does not know—falling down and crying out, That's my cross! That is where I belong!

And then I make the third identification, which is implied in the second and may be a part of it: my personal identification of devotion to Christ, the identification of worship. It breathes in many songs, but unless it breathes in the heart, the songs have a brassy sound. (118)

Crites describes this process as a "reawakening":

...a conversion or a social revolution that actually transforms consciousness requires a traumatic change in a man's [sic.] story. The stories within which he has awakened to consciousness must be undermined, and in the identification of his personal story through a new story both the drama of his experience and his style of action must be reoriented. Conversion is reawakening, a second awakening of consciousness. . . . Not only his past and future, but the very cosmos in which he lives is strung in a new way. (83)

While this "reawakening" may be initiated by one's losing a theological debate and accepting a new set of doctrinal propositions (as is often the case in typical Church of Christ evangelism), I would argue that a more satisfactory impetus for conversion is provided by hearing the Gospel in such as way that it collides with our personal stories.[22] The result is a new identity —a Christian identity, which has been described as "the adventure of a meeting with Jesus Christ, of a life shared with Him on a path which leads Him to the cross" (Bühler:27). In fact, this illuminates the meaning of discipleship, as Stroup observes:

A proper understanding of the identity of Jesus Christ goes hand in hand with the question of discipleship. To understand who Jesus is means that one must come to terms with the cross that gives him his identity and characterizes the nature of Christian discipleship. (220)

Narrative and the Reshaping of Identity

Having shaped their Christian identities around their acceptance of the Church's doctrinal distinctives, many members of the Church of Christ find themselves shaken to the core when the Church reconsiders and or even reverses its position on doctrinal issues.[23] I wish to contend that for Christians whose identities have been deficiently reckoned doctrinally (rather than christologically), a reshaping of identity is possible. A Christian can, by means of narrative collisions experience a transformation of identity.[24] An example of how transformation can come to a person who experiences a narrative collision may be seen in the following Old Testament story.

An Illustration from David's Life

The writer of 2 Samuel tells an unflattering story about king David (11:1-27) beginning with these suspicious words: "In the spring of the year, the time when kings go out to battle, David sent Joab with his officers and all Israel with him; they ravaged the Ammonites, and besieged Rabbah. But David remained in Jerusalem." Immediately, a red flag goes up in the reader's mind —David is in the wrong place; shouldn't he be on the battlefield? Indeed he should, as the unfolding dark tale reveals. Late one day, David arose from his couch and, in apparent boredom, took a stroll on his palace roof. From that vantage point he saw a very beautiful woman bathing. Inquiring after her, he found that she was Bathsheba the wife of Uriah, one of his soldiers. He called for her and they had sexual intercourse. Their illicit affair would not be easily hidden, though, because she became pregnant. Upon hearing that news, David summoned Uriah and encouraged (ordered?) him to go home. Rather than sleeping with his wife, as the compromised king had hoped, the honorable Uriah slept alone in David's palace. When David found out his plan had failed, he asked Uriah to explain his actions. Uriah's response underscored his noble character. As long as the holy ark and the army of God's people were in harm's way, Uriah explained, he would not treat himself to the pleasures of home. That night David got him drunk. Perhaps David was hoping the inebriated soldier would forget himself and stumble home for sexual favors; but he didn't. Instead, Uriah stayed with the king's servants. So, the next day the desperate king sent Uriah back to the battlefield with secret orders for his commander to ensure his death in an apparent accident. Commander Joab obeyed, and Uriah died needlessly in an act of betrayal. Soon after, David took Bathsheba to be his wife. Not surprisingly, the writer asserted: "The thing that David had done displeased the Lord."

In the story, God chose to use a collision of narratives to bring David to repentance. The Lord sent the prophet Nathan to the backslidden king — armed only with this story:

> There were two men in a certain city, the one rich and the other poor. The rich man had very many flocks and herds; but the poor man had nothing but one little ewe lamb, which he had bought. He brought it up, and it grew up with him and with his children; it used to eat of his meager fare, and drank from his cup, and lie in his bosom, and it was like a daughter to him. Now there came a traveler to the rich man, and he was loath to take from his own flock or herd to prepare for the wayfarer who had come to him; but he took the poor man's lamb, and prepared that for the guest who had come to him. (2 Samuel 12:1b-4)

David listened with genuine empathy to the story. It was one that resonated with him on many levels. Having been a shepherd, he no doubt knew what it was to have a pet lamb. Having been the baby in his family, he no doubt knew what it was to be bullied. Having been the object of Saul's jealous rage, he knew what it was to be unfairly treated. In righteous indignation he said to Nathan: "As the Lord lives, the man who has done this deserves to die!" No sooner did those words burst from the king's mouth, Nathan fired back: "You are the man!" The prophet then explained to David that by killing Uriah and marrying his wife, he was guilty of despising the word of the Lord and doing evil in God's sight. The result? David repented. "I have sinned," he painfully acknowledged.

The prophet could have taken a different tact; he could have simply wagged an accusing finger while saying: "Shame on you! By lusting after Bathsheba you broke the tenth commandment; by sleeping with her you broke the seventh commandment; by attempting to cover your sin you broke the ninth commandment; and by having Uriah killed you broke the sixth commandment!" And it may have had the same outcome; but that is unlikely. It seems that David had justified his actions and was not prepared to admit any wrongdoing when Nathan arrived. He had fallen prey to the power of self-deception.[25]

The genius of Nathan's approach was that it facilitated an identification process. As David listened to the story he identified with the victim (Foreman's Type 2). But as Nathan challenged that interpretation ("You are the man!"), the story then collided with David's personal story. It shattered his self-deception.[26] In so doing, it caused David to reevaluate his identity (Foreman's Type 4 identification —Person A thinks he or she is person B and then discovers he or she is actually A, and accepts it). This identification opened the door for David to make the next type of identification (Type 5 —Person A knows he or she is person A and either rejoices or regrets it). That regret motivated David to meet the requirements necessary to regain proper standing with God (namely, to offer to God "a broken spirit" because "a broken and contrite heart. . . God. . . will not despise" Psalm 51:17). At the end of this identification process David's personal identity was reshaped (presumably as a person after God's own heart —Acts 13:26).

Application

In the same way, a Christian whose identity has been deficiently based in a church's doctrinal distinctives can (and I believe, should) be reshaped by encountering the person of Jesus through narrative collisions with the Gospel. Two New Testament examples may be helpful in clarifying my intention.

The Son of Thunder becomes the Apostle of Love

One of Jesus' closest friends was John, brother of James, son of Zebedee. Although the evangelists say relatively little about him, Luke tells a story that gives a fairly strong image of John's character. After Jesus "set his face to go to Jerusalem" (Luke 9:51), he encountered opposition from some bigoted Samaritans. Notice John's reaction:

> On their way, they entered a village of the Samaritans, to make ready for him; but they did not receive him, because his face was set toward Jerusalem. When his disciples James and John saw it, they said, "Lord, do you want us to command fire to come down from heaven and consume them?" But he turned and rebuked them. (Luke 9:52-55)

When we combine this extreme reaction with Mark's comment that it was to these brothers that Jesus "gave the name Boanerges, that is, `Sons of Thunder'" (Mark 3:17), it seems reasonable to assume John had a rather explosive temper. At that time in his life, John seems to have felt that the opponents of Jesus didn't deserve to live! Yet, John's lasting reputation among the early Christians is not as the "Son of Thunder" but as the "apostle of love." What made the difference? For John, the difference was in what he witnessed in the life of his Rabbi and, ultimately, what he saw at the cross; the self-giving love exemplified by Jesus in the crucifixion became John's paradigm for human interaction: "We know love by this, that He laid down His life for us —and we ought to lay down our lives for one another" (1 John 3:16). For John, loving others became the principal thing (3:11). To hate was to show oneself a murderer without hope of eternal life (3:15). When John's story collided with Jesus' story (lived out in his presence) he was changed.

A Murderer becomes a Missionary

The story of Saul of Taursus is one of the most dramatic examples of conversion in all of the New Testament. We first encounter him approving of the murder of Stephen (Acts 8:1). We then are led to imagine his fanatical exploits as he "ravages the church" (8:3) and "breathes out murder against the disciples" of Jesus (9:1). We reluctantly travel with him the road to Damascus, dreading to see him fulfill his intentions when he arrives (9:1-3). His reputation preceded him to that distant city and the disciples there worried of being taken captive by him (9:13-14). Then, in a momentary flash of a blinding light, Saul was stopped in his tracks. He met the risen Lord by means of a heavenly vision, and from henceforth was a dogged defender of "the Way" and a devoted disciple of Jesus. What brought about the change? It was simply that Saul's story collided with the story of Jesus. The result was a new —a completely new —personal identity (which even included a new name!). He explained:

> even though I, too, have reason for confidence in the flesh. If anyone has reason to be confident in the flesh, I have more: circumcised the eighth day, a member of the people of Israel, of the tribe of Benjamin, a Hebrew born of Hebrews; as to the law, a Pharisee; as to zeal, a persecutor of the church; as to righteousness under the law, blameless. Yet whatever gains I had, these I have come to regard as loss because of Christ. More than that, I regard everything as loss because of the surpassing value of knowing Christ Jesus my Lord. For his sake I have suffered the loss of all things, and I regard them as rubbish, in order that I may gain Christ. (Philippians 3:4-8)

From the time of his conversion until his death, Saul (whose name was changed to Paul) was a missionary for the cause he had originally sought to eradicate. This was the lasting result of the jarring collision that occurred when his story encountered the Gospel story. It was to that story that Paul frequently referred when attempting to persuade Christians to reform their lives (see Romans 1:16; Romans 5:6-11; 1 Corinthians 15:1-8; Galatians 2:20; Philippians 2:5-11; et al.).

Summary and Trajectory

In this chapter I have suggested that the identity crisis in the Church of Christ is, in large measure, an unfortunate legacy of its Enlightenment roots. Evidence of the crisis is seen in the troubling reality that while some people concur with the major doctrines of Christianity (and may even be Christians in name for many years), yet they show little evidence of true faith. This is because there has been, in them, a lack of true identification. And, as Foreman put it: "Mental assent is not identification. Assent may or may not be existential, identification must be" (118). Identification requires an exercise of the human will. Whereas acceptance of doctrinal distinctives is a weak impetus for identification, the collision of my personal story with the Gospel story is a strong catalyst for identity-shaping.

Two Clarifications

As I conclude this chapter, I wish to state two clarifications raised by my reading of Charles Campbell's Preaching Jesus: New Directions for Homiletics in Hans Frei's Postliberal Theology. The first relates to my focus upon "personal" identity. Campbell (developing Frei's theology) observes that in much of contemporary narrative homiletics, "Christian faith all too easily gets relegated to the private realm" (143). He further argues that "the preacher's task must be seen, not as that of creating experiential events for individual hearers, but rather as that of building up the church" (221). I agree on both counts. In fact, it is not through the individual, but the church that "the wisdom of God in its rich variety might now be made known" (Ephesians 3:10). So, this project's emphasis on "personal" identity is not to be taken as an argument for "lone ranger" Christianity. The Christian religion is not simply a matter of individuals standing alone before their God. Jesus himself created a community of his followers and it is in community that the Christian faith is interpreted, confessed and lived.

At the same time, though, each Christian, like Bob, struggles individually with his or her faith and is called as an individual to make identity-shaping identifications with Jesus. As Paul said: "It is he whom we proclaim, warning everyone and teaching everyone in all wisdom, so that we may present everyone mature in Christ" (Colossians 1:28, emphasis added). The church is not a community of flat sameness in which individuality completely dissolves.[27] Each member is individually gifted and brings something unique to the community of faith (see Romans 14; 1 Corinthians 12; Ephesians 41-16; et al.). There is room for both corporate and personal identity in the church. Stroup put it well:

> In Christian faith it is not just that the individual discovers his or her personal identity in the narrative history of the community. In Christian faith both the individual and the community look to the narrative history of Jesus of Nazareth in order to discover the true meaning of their respective identities. (168)

Both the community and its members need an identity shaped by Christology, rather than doctrinal distinctives. This hermeneutical task is best accomplished within the context of the Christian community.[28] This project's proposed act of ministry is intended to be executed within the communal setting of a class study.

Second, this chapter's emphasis on "story" and the experiential "collision" between personal identity stories and the story of Jesus is not meant to suggest that form is more important than content. I concur with Campbell that story is "important because it is the vehicle through which the gospels render the identity of Jesus of Nazareth, who has been raised from the dead and seeks today to form a people who follow his way" (190). While I appreciate the power of story, and acknowledge that it functions more effectively in shaping identity than does giving mental assent to propositional doctrinal statements, I do not believe that just any story will do, or that stories containing so-called "Christ-figures" can replace Gospel proclamation. I consider story to be essential for identity-shaping because it is true to human experience (and indeed changes and even creates human experiences), and it is the form in which the Gospel comes to us.

In the next chapter, I will explore the message of the Gospel of Luke-Acts and suggest that it serves as an appropriate meeting place for us to encounter Jesus in an identity-shaping way.

CHAPTER 4

THE IDENTITY OF JESUS IN THE GOSPEL OF LUKE

Introduction

Luke's story of Jesus is firmly rooted in a real world of politics and history. References to Caesars, local kings, governors and decrees abound in Luke-Acts. Jesus was born miles away from his home because of the odd decree of Augustus Caesar; his forerunner was beheaded by the capricious order of King Herod, and his own fate was sealed by the decision of a governor who was likely more concerned with avoiding a riot than serving justice (Luke 2:1; 3:19; 9:9; 23:13-25). Although there has been considerable discussion regarding the veracity of some of Luke's historical statements, there is no doubt that he intended his story to be understood as having occurred in real time and among real people (Tiede:65-67). This is no fantasy.

Unlike the other Gospels, Luke begins with a brief preface that indicates the author's intention to lead his original reader —Theophilus —to a better understanding of the story of Jesus (a story Theophilus already has heard, at least cursorily):

> Since many have undertaken to set down an orderly account of the events that have been fulfilled among us, just as they were handed on to us by those who from the beginning were eyewitnesses and servants of the word. I too decided, after investigating everything carefully from the very first, to write an orderly account for you, most excellent Theophilus, so that you might know the truth concerning the things about which you have been instructed. (Luke 1:1-4)

The book of Acts is likewise addressed to Theophilus and its preface promises to continue the story that began with Jesus:

> In the first book, Theophilus, I wrote about all that Jesus did and taught from the beginning until the day he was taken up to heaven,

> after giving instructions through the Holy Spirit to the apostles whom he had chosen. (Acts 1:1-2)

Of Theophilus we know nothing, but his title "most excellent" encourages speculation that he was a Roman official (see also Acts 23:26). Why such a person should need Luke-Acts, is also unknown; it is possible that the books were written as an apology —a work designed to provide him with sufficient background to deliver a favorable judgment regarding the legal status of Christianity in the Roman world. Of course, we might with equal imagination suppose Theophilus was someone Luke was attempting to lead to personal, Christian conversion. Regardless of whether Luke-Acts was initially intended to serve as an apology or as an evangelistic tract, it comprises approximately one quarter of the Christian Canon and has touched millions of lives in the two millennia since Theophilus first read its words.

Jesus as Savior in Luke

Jesus is presented in Luke-Acts as "Savior." This identity is foreshadowed in the events preceding and surrounding his birth. At the circumcision and naming ceremony of Jesus' forerunner, John, his father Zechariah prophesied, "Blessed be the Lord God of Israel, for he has looked favorably on his people and redeemed them. He has raised up a mighty savior for us in the house of his servant David" (Luke 1:68-69). Three months later, Jesus' birth is announced to startled shepherds by joyful angels: "to you is born this day in the city of David a Savior, who is the Messiah, the Lord" (Luke 2:11). This emphasis on salvation is maintained throughout the narrative. A man named Simeon is told by the Holy Spirit that he would not die until he saw "the Lord's Messiah" (Luke 2:26). Finally, on the occasion of Jesus' circumcision, the aged Simeon sees the baby Jesus in the temple and exclaims:

> Master, now you are dismissing your servant in peace, according to your word; for my eyes have seen your salvation, which you have prepared in the presence of all peoples, a light for the revelation to the Gentiles and for glory to your people Israel. (Luke 2:29-32)

Simeon recognized Jesus as the Messiah, the one through whom God's promised salvation would come.

This insight was also shared by the elderly prophetess Anna who, after seeing the baby, "began to praise God and to speak about the child to all who were looking for the redemption of Jerusalem" (Luke 2:38, emphasis added).

Luke sets the context for John's preparatory ministry by drawing upon the language of Isaiah 40:

> The voice of one crying out in the wilderness: Prepare the way of the Lord; make his paths straight. Every valley shall be filled, and every mountain and hill shall be made low, and the crooked shall be made straight, and the rough ways made smooth. (Luke 3:4-5)

Ideally, all this preparation was to culminate in the ultimate goal: "and all flesh shall see the salvation of God" (Luke 3:6). John "prepared the way" so that in Jesus humanity could experience salvation.

Inverted Values

One of the most dramatic indications of humanity's need for a savior is in the inverted values that prevail in human society, even among many who view themselves as pious. Constantly, through both his actions and words, Jesus criticizes and corrects the values of lost humanity. In the most unambiguous terms, Jesus affirmed, "what is prized by human beings is an abomination in the sight of God" (Luke 16:15b). As Luke sees it, human beings prize highly material riches and hierarchical human relationships. The savior critiques and corrects these misplaced values.

Material riches

Although economic prosperity is often viewed as a sign of God's favor and the lack of material wealth as an indication of divine displeasure, Luke's Gospel suggests otherwise. The reversal of this value begins even before Jesus' birth is described. When the Savior's mother is blessed by John's mother, Elizabeth, she responds with a song of praise (in the tradition of Hannah —1 Samuel 2:1-10). She interprets God's choice of her as an indication that "[God] has brought down the powerful from their thrones, and lifted up the lowly; he has filled the hungry with good things, and sent the rich away empty" (Luke 1:52-53). Indeed, the savior is born to a poor family, bedded down in a feeding trough, and first welcomed into the world by a rag-tag group of lowly shepherds (Luke 2:7-16). Because of their poverty, when the time came for Jesus' family to "present" him before the Lord they offered a sacrifice of two doves instead of the usual offering of a lamb and a pigeon (Leviticus 12:8).

When the people came to John —ostensibly to learn how to prepare for the coming Messiah —he demanded that they "Bear fruits worthy of repentance!" (Luke 3:7). When they requested clarification, he responded: "Whoever has two coats must share with anyone who has none; and whoever has food, must do likewise" (vs. 11). He told tax collectors to collect only what was prescribed (undercutting their ability to become wealthy at the expense of others), and he told soldiers to be content with their wages rather than to bully people out of more money. Repentance, therefore, had an economic dimension. And this perspective is part of the tapestry that forms the backdrop of expectancy for Jesus' ministry.

The Isaianic prophecy that served as Jesus' commencement address and ministerial charter, plainly stated that he was anointed by God "to bring good news to the poor" (Luke 4:18). So we are not surprised to hear him preach: "Blessed are you who are poor, for yours is the kingdom of God" or to see that he lives the life of an itinerant preacher who has "nowhere to lay his head" (Luke 6:20; 9:58). But Jesus also has a strong message about the dangers of wealth: "Woe to you who are rich," he said, "for you have received your consolation" (Luke 6:24). He warned that riches can hinder a person from bearing fruit for God (Luke 8:14), and spoke higher praise for the paltry gift given by a poor widow into the temple treasury than for all the excessive gifts deposited by rich people (Luke 21:1-4). Two of his parables were overtly critical of people who put their trust in riches (Luke 12:16-21; 16:19-31). When approached for salvation by a religious, yet wealthy, individual Jesus unflinchingly required that he sell all he had and give the proceeds to the poor (Luke 18:18-23). When the man chose to keep his money and go away unsaved, Jesus let him go, pointing out that it is "easier for a camel to go through the eye of a needle than for someone who is rich to enter the kingdom of God" (Luke 18:24).

His actions and teaching converge in this matter; he neither pursued personal wealth, nor showed favoritism toward those who had it. Imitating him, his disciples left their wealth behind to follow him (Luke 5:11; 5:27-28; 18:28) and he urged them to simply subsist on handouts from those with whom they shared the good news of the kingdom (Luke 9:1-4; 10:1-9). For Jesus, being "rich toward God" is of supreme importance (Luke 12:21).

Hierarchical human relationships

From the very beginning of the Gospel, it is obvious that the Messiah's story is framed by a different set of social values. The Lukan narrative begins, not with a contemplative gaze back into a surreal era of eternal existence and creative activity, as does the Gospel of John, nor does it begin with a hurried look at the wilderness ministry of the rough-and-tumble John baptizing all the people of Jerusalem, as it does in Mark. Instead, Luke begins by introducing us to a couple of social misfits. Although the evangelist tells us they are righteous before God, we are sure society has long ago passed a contrary judgment; after all, "they had no children, because Elizabeth was barren, and both were getting on in years" (Luke 1:7). There were plenty of people in the community who would readily remind Zechariah and Elizabeth that "children are a heritage from God," and "a reward" to those who keep God's covenant

(Psalm 127:3; Deuteronomy 28:1-6). Yet, to them comes the amazing news —they would bear a son who would prepare the people for the coming Messiah! Imagine the excitement in Elizabeth's voice when she responded to the news of her pregnancy by saying, "This is what the Lord has done for me when he looked favorably on me and took away the disgrace I have endured among my people" (Luke 1:25).

Actually, this Gospel is filled with outcasts and misfits: there is Anna the widow (widowhood is usually a sign of God-forsakenness) who prophesies (Luke 2:36-38); the "sinful" woman who demonstrates greater love than the Pharisee (Luke 7:36-50); the bent woman who receives Jesus' special notice (Luke 13:10-17); the tax collector who goes home justified (Luke 18:9-14); and the criminal who alone understands that Jesus' death on the cross would not keep him from coming into his kingdom —something even the disciples had missed (Luke 23:42).

The whole social hierarchy is challenged from beginning to end! The Messiah enters the world through the womb of a virgin girl and is bedded down in a manger of hay (Luke 1:27; 2:7); he dies naked before the world and is buried in a borrowed tomb (Luke 23:34,53). Although anointed by God and destined for royal rule, Jesus never asserts privilege, never plays by the rules of the shame and honor game, and never sought a place of social standing. He had both female and male disciples (Luke 8:1-3); and he healed the poor as well as the rich (Luke 8:40-56). He touched the untouchables, ate with the sinners, held children up as model citizens of the kingdom, and allowed his public ministry to be underwritten from the purses of women (Luke 5:13; 5:30; 18:16; 8:3).

Even the family —the most basic set of human relationships —is recast in the light of Jesus' kingdom agenda, which, he said would set "father against son and son against father, mother against daughter and daughter against mother" (Luke 12:53). He challenged those who would follow him to first sit down and count the cost. It was, he explained, extremely high: "Whoever comes to me and does not hate father and mother, wife and children, brothers and sisters, yes even life itself, cannot be my disciple" (Luke 14:26). Clearly, human society is thoroughly challenged by this savior.

"He Eats with Sinners!"

Jesus' critique of human hierarchies is especially pronounced in his dining practices and his advice to a dinner host:

> When you give a luncheon or a dinner, do not invite your friends or your brothers or your relatives or rich neighbors, in case they may invite you in return, and you will be repaid. But when you give a

> banquet, invite the poor, the crippled, the lame, and the blind. And you will be blessed, because they cannot repay you, for you will be repaid at the resurrection of the righteous. (Luke 14:12-14)

In a society where one's social standing is displayed by the importance of those one invites to a banquet, this guest list is particularly subversive. No doubt Jesus' host was wondering: "What will the community think of my place in the hierarchy if the only people I invite to dinner are those who, by virtue of their poverty and infirmity, are excluded from the hierarchy? I will be seen as one who has no honor!" The social tension Jesus created by his table fellowship was enormous. Joel Green explains:

> In the ancient Mediterranean world, mealtime was a social event whose significance far outdistanced the need to satisfy one's hunger. To welcome people at the table became tantamount to extending to them intimacy, solidarity, acceptance; table companions were treated as though they were of one's extended family. Sharing food, encoded messages about hierarchy, inclusion and exclusion, boundaries and crossing boundaries. (Green:87)

So, Jesus undercut established human hierarchies by his open association with everyone. Not only did he eat with the rich and poor, but also with religiously meticulous Pharisees (Luke 7:36) and religiously outcast tax collectors (Luke 5:29). In fact, by eating with more than five thousand, Jesus pitched the entire table-fellowship system into a cocked hat (Green:87). But Jesus does this deliberately. He understood the rules of table fellowship and exploited them: "The very people excluded from the table of the holy, he welcomes, and in so doing he serves as their physician (5:31) and extends to them salvation (19:9-10)" (Green:88).

The kingdom of children, mustard plants, and leaven

Jesus inverted the existing power structures. He asserted that in the kingdom, the first are to be last and the last are to be first (Luke 13:30); the "least among all of you is the greatest" (Luke 9:48b); moreover, when his disciples attempted to stop people from bringing their infants to Jesus, he chastised them by saying,

> Let the little children come to me and do not stop them; for it is to such as these that the kingdom of heaven belongs. Truly I tell you, whoever does not receive the kingdom of God as a little child will never enter it. (Luke 18:16-17)

No one was more powerless in the society of Jesus' day than children. The practice of abandoning unwanted babies to the elements and wild animals was common and underscored their lack of status. A child was literally "nothing, a nobody, a nonperson in the Mediterranean world"

(Crossan, 1994:64). Hence, "a Kingdom of Children is a Kingdom of Nobodies" (Crossan, 1994:64). So powerless were they that if a child received anything, it would come as a gift; that seems to be the point Jesus was attempting to get across: people enter the kingdom not because they deserve to, but because it is given to them!

The kingdom itself is described in wonderfully paradoxical images. Rather than being a nationalistic entity that conquers by the exercise of great military might, the kingdom is,

> ...like a mustard seed, which a man took and put in his garden; and it grew and became a large tree, and the birds of the air nested in its branches. And again He said, To what shall I liken the kingdom of God? It is like leaven, which a woman took and hid in three measures of meal till it was all leavened. (Luke 13:19-21)

These two images apparently point in two complementary directions. Not only do they speak of the way the kingdom would progress from a modest beginning to a broad, expansive reality, they also describe a kingdom whose growth would not be universally welcomed. Crossan explains:

> The point, in other words, is not just that the mustard plant starts as a proverbially small seed and grows into a shrub of three, or four, or even more feet in height. It is that it tends to take over where it is not wanted, that it tends to get out of control, and that it tends to attract birds within cultivated areas, where they are not particularly desired. (Crossan, 1994:65)

So the mustard plant imagery may well be a disconcerting picture that suggests not everyone will stand and applaud the kingdom's progress. And, from the standpoint of those who seek a kingdom that endorses the fleshly values of riches and social status, this kingdom will actually be opposed because of the spiritual riffraff it attracts (Luke 7:34).

The second image of leaven is likely intended to convey similar tension. Leaven was already used by Jesus as a picturesque metaphor for the insidious way hypocrisy works to corrupt a person's heart. "Be on your guard against the yeast of the Pharisees, which is hypocrisy" (Luke 12:1). Leaven is a force that, once buried in a lump of dough, is unstoppable. It works invisibly until the entire lump is finally affected. Like it or not, the kingdom's influence will be felt!

Thus, in all these ways, the point is made and graphically underlined: Jesus as Savior brings a holistic salvation that is understood,

> in the most all-encompassing way possible. Luke holds together what the contemporary church has often partitioned into discordant

elements: empowering the disadvantaged, seeking the lost, reconciling person's across social lines, calling people to repentance, healing the sick, forgiving sins, initiating people into the community of God's people. (Green:136)

Evaluations of Jesus by Lukan Characters

In addition to this thematic look at Jesus as savior, it may also be helpful to consider how the characters in Luke see Jesus and to ponder how their impressions impact our understanding of his identity.

The Evaluations of Supernatural Characters

The evangelist includes evaluations of Jesus' identity from supernatural sources. Their evaluations are diverse yet consistent. The angel Gabriel announces to Mary that she will conceive and bear a son, who is to be named Jesus. The messenger continued:

> He will be great, and will be called the Son of the Most High, and the Lord God will give to him the throne of his ancestor David. He will reign over the house of Jacob forever and of his kingdom there will be no end. (Luke 1:31-33)

After Mary questioned how she, a virgin, could bear a child, Gabriel assured her that the Holy Spirit would perform the miracle. As a consequence, said the messenger, "the child to be born would be holy; he will be called the Son of God" (1:35). Although the designation "son of God" could be used to refer to one holding royal office (Psalm 2:7), or to a member of the Israelite nation (Hosea 11:1), this context implies an intimate, unique relationship with God.

On the night of Jesus' birth an angel announced to startled shepherds: "Do not be afraid; for see —I am bringing you good news of great joy for all the people: to you is born this day in the city of David a Savior, who is the Messiah, the Lord" (2:10-11). In other words, the infant Jesus was considered by the messenger to be the long-anticipated prophet like Moses, priest like Melchizedek, and king from David's lineage (Deuteronomy 18:15; Psalm 110:4; Hebrews 5:6; Isaiah 9:7). Angels later announced his resurrection (Luke 24:4-7), and still later assured the disciples who witnessed his ascension that he "will come in the same way as you saw him go into heaven" (Acts 1:11).

On two occasions, an audible voice from heaven states what is obviously intended to be taken as God's evaluation of Jesus: "You are my Son, the Beloved; with you I am well pleased" and "This is my Son, my Chosen; listen to him!" (Luke 3:22; 9:35). Luke ends —and Acts begins —with Jesus ascending to the same heavenly realm as God (Luke 24:51; Acts 1:9).

His presence there is confirmed by Stephen's claim that he saw the "heavens opened and the Son of Man standing on the right hand of God!" (Acts 7:56). So it is not a complete surprise to hear Jesus speak to Saul of Tarsus, to Annanias, or to Peter from that other-worldly place (Acts 9:4; 10; 10:13; 18:9). The Jesus who speaks from heaven in these various and curious texts does so from a perspective consistent with all other supernatural evaluations.

In Luke, Jesus encounters the forces of supernatural evil in two forms: in the person of the devil who tempts him in the wilderness (Luke 4:1-13), and in demon-possessed humans (and people afflicted with "evil spirits"). In the first case, the devil appears to know Jesus' true identity, and attempts to persuade him to act contrary to it. Joel Green gives this summary of the temptation scene:

> With varying degrees of deceit, then, the devil strikes at the heart of what it means for Jesus to be "Son of God" in the Lukan narrative — namely, the one who would carry out his mission in absolute allegiance to God, serve without compromise God's redemptive purpose, and as God's agent rule his everlasting kingdom. (Green: 33)

At the end of this encounter, Luke writes: "When the devil had finished all this tempting, he left him until an opportune time," which, as it turns out, doesn't occur until near the end of the Gospel. The opportunity arrives in the form and person of a disenchanted disciple: "Satan entered Judas" who "watched for an opportunity to hand Jesus over to" the chief priests and teachers of the law (Luke 4:13; 22:2,6).

In the second case, the demons and evil spirits that inhabited and terrorized certain humans recognized Jesus and submitted to his commands. A demonic in Capernaum screams at Jesus: "Let us alone! What have you to do with us, Jesus of Nazareth? Have you come to destroy us? I know who you are, the Holy One of God" (Luke 4:34). According to Luke, this evaluation is shared by many other demons who shout as they are also being exorcised: "You are the Son of God!" (Luke 4:40).

As the church continued Jesus' mission, it too encountered demonic forces and practiced exorcism (Acts 5:16; 8:7; 16:16; 19:12). When we are allowed to hear their testimony in Acts, evil spirits speak in terms consistent with the perspective of the demons in Luke. They know who Jesus is and submit to his power that is at work among his true followers. Two instances are noteworthy. In the first case, the spirit of divination that Paul and Silas encountered in Philippi enabled a slave girl to proclaim: "These men are slaves of the Most High God, who proclaim to you a way of salvation" and submitted to Paul's command: "I order you in the name of Jesus Christ to come out of her" (Acts 16:17-18). In the second case, when some unbelieving Jews attempted to cast out evil spirits "by the Jesus whom Paul proclaims," the spirit responded: "Jesus I know, and Paul I know; but who are you?" (Acts 19:15). Because they were not followers of the Lord, they were unable to exorcise; instead, they were overpowered by the possessed man and fled from the scene naked and bleeding (Acts 19:16).

It is obvious that the evangelist intends for his reader to infer that it is by supernatural guidance that human characters such as Elizabeth, Simeon, and Anna all confess in their own ways that Jesus is the Messiah (namely, "my Lord," "salvation" and the one bringing "the redemption of Jerusalem" —Luke 1:43; 2:30; 2:38). So, in Luke-Acts, the identity of Jesus is known by supernatural forces both good and evil: Jesus is God's Holy Son, the one who brings salvation (i.e., the Messiah).

The Evaluations of the Roman Authorities

Roman authorities figure occasionally in the story. Their view of Jesus is somewhat mixed. There is, on the one hand, an unnamed Centurion who "amazed" Jesus and about whom the Lord said: "not even in Israel have I found such faith" (Luke 7:9); on the other hand, there are the rough-cut soldiers who sarcastically scoffed at Jesus as he hung on the cross: "If you are the King of the Jews, save yourself!" (Luke 23:37).

For Herod, Jesus apparently was a frightening curiosity. After he beheaded John, he began hearing stories about Jesus and wondered if John had been raised from the dead (Luke 9:7-9). Stories of Jesus' miracles intrigued him; he hoped to see Jesus work some magic for him. When Pilate sent Jesus to Herod, though, Jesus refused to perform and remained silent. Frustrated, Herod mocked him and sent him back to the governor (Luke 23:6-11). On one occasion the Pharisees tell Jesus: "Get away from here [Galilee], for Herod wants to kill you" (Luke 13:31). Given what we have just observed about Herod, though, this seems to be a false testimony —perhaps a lie designed to intimidate Jesus. Jesus, probably seeing through their deceit, threw the ball back into their court: "Go and tell that fox for me, Listen, I am casting out demons and performing cures today and tomorrow, and on the third day I finish my work. . . " (Luke 13:32). In other words, Jesus will leave the region, but on God's timetable and no one else's. If anything, their taking that message to Herod would have resulted in making Jesus even more interesting to Herod, rather than less so.

Pilate, the Roman governor of Jerusalem, examines Jesus closely, and repeatedly pronounces him innocent:

> You brought me this man as one who was perverting the people; and here I have examined him in your presence and have not found him guilty of any of your charges against him. Neither has Herod, for he sent him back to us. Indeed, he has done nothing to deserve death. (Luke 23:14-15)

Three times he urged the Jewish leaders to drop their trumped up charges so Jesus could be released; every time they grew increasingly antagonistic. Finally, when it was obvious that the only way to avoid an all-out riot was to deliver Jesus to death, he acquiesced to their demand (Luke 23:3-25). Luke seems to have used this episode not only to emphasize Jesus' innocence, but to exonerate the Romans from malicious blame in the death of Jesus. In fact, in Acts 4:28 the actions of Pilate and Herod are credited to the Sovereign will of God: they did "whatever [God's] hand and [God's] plan had predestined to take place." With the exception of Herod who slew James and imprisoned Peter to gain favor with his Jewish subjects (Acts 12), the Roman authorities throughout Acts appear neutral or positively disposed toward Jesus' followers. If anything, they are curious about this new religion and are its potential converts (Acts 24:24-25; 26:1-29).

The Evaluations of the Jewish Leaders

The story of Jesus is filled with references to his interaction with the spiritual leaders of the Jewish people. These leaders are variously described as "teachers," "scribes and Pharisees," "lawyers," "Sadducees," "synagogue leaders," "chief priests," "elders," and "council members". They represent two different theological parties —Sadducees and Pharisees. The former group was numerically smaller, and yet (apparently) controlled the official priestly caste (Acts 5:17). Luke reports that the Sadducees "say there is no resurrection" "or angel, or spirit" (Luke 20:27; Acts 23:8). The latter group was much larger; they were essentially viewed as defenders of popular orthodoxy (although not actually possessing any positional authority, they acted as leaders and are thus treated in this section; see Tannehill:170). This being the case, Jesus had more encounters and confrontations with Pharisees.

Although the Pharisees, as a class, were not totally closed to the teachings of Jesus (some became believers —see Acts 15:5), they are consistently suspicious and critical of him. From the first encounter, when they accuse him of blasphemy for claiming to forgive sins (Luke 5:21), to the last when they angrily tell him: "order your disciples to stop" singing "Blessed is the king who comes in the name of the Lord! Peace in heaven, and glory in the highest heaven" (Luke 19:38-39), the Pharisees dog Jesus' every move. They have three major complaints against him:

1. He "forgives sins" (e.g., Luke 5:21; 7:49).

2. He socializes with "sinners" (e.g., Luke 5:30, 15:1-2);

3. He heals on the Sabbath day (e.g., 6:7-11; 13:14).

Each of these areas of contention provides Jesus with an opportunity to correct a common misunderstanding prevalent in popular piety. First, he deals with the question of forgiveness from two sides. On the first side, he seems to be saying that he does in fact have the divine authority to forgive sins because he is the "Son of Man" (Luke 5:24). On the other side, he teaches that forgiveness is not solely a divine prerogative, it is also enjoined upon humans (Luke 6:37; 11:4) and so he models it for the community (Luke 23:34).

Second, he handles the matter of table fellowship by agreeing with the Pharisees that those with whom he eats are sinners and then by challenging them to see that as sinners they need him like a sick person needs a physician (Luke 5:31). Finally, although he in no way legitimizes unauthorized work on the Sabbath, he critiques the Pharisees' double standard; they would lead a donkey from its stall to water on the Sabbath, but they call in question the appropriateness of his healing on the Sabbath. He wishes them to see that since they were right to show compassion to their animals, he was certainly within the law to show compassion to humans on the Sabbath. They would do well to follow his example. Additionally, he asserts that he as "the Son of Man (a title with Messianic significance) is lord of the Sabbath" (Luke 6:5). The Pharisees are at cross-purposes with Jesus throughout the story and their misguided piety serves as a convenient starting point for much of his teaching regarding the kingdom of God (see Luke 11:37-44; 11:53-12:1; 18:10-14).

For all their antagonism, though, they seem to be relatively harmless; some are eventually brought to faith in Jesus by the early church (Acts 15:5). Unfortunately, they had a difficult time giving up their reliance on external rituals as a means of obtaining a right-standing before God (Acts 15:1). This posed a challenge to the early church that required a general convention, and received much attention in Paul's writings (see Acts 15; Galatians; et al.).

Once Jesus arrived in Jerusalem, the Pharisees disappeared from the Lukan stage. In their place as his adversaries are the elders, chief priests, and their scribes. Although the Pharisees had been at times infuriated by what they didn't like about Jesus, and even "discussed with one another what they might do to" him (Luke 6:11), it was the leaders in Jerusalem who sought his death and paid Judas to betray him into their hands (Luke 22:1-6). They immediately demanded that he tell them by what authority he acted and taught (Acts 20:2). In short order they concluded he was deserving of death and set in motion the diabolical plan to achieve that objective (Luke 20:19; 22:1-2; 22:66-71; 23:1-2; 13-23). With hardened hearts they pressured the Roman authorities to execute him; they even went so far as to mock him while he was in the throes of death (Luke 23:35).

While the fledgling church began to find its legs, it was the priests, elders and Sadducees who sought to stop it (Acts 4:1; 23; 5:24). With the same passion that had driven them to murder Jesus, they attempted to silence the church. They were greatly annoyed at the teaching that "in Jesus there is the resurrection from the dead" (Acts 4:2). They were the ones who granted authority to Saul of Tarsus to travel as far north as Damascus to "bind all who invoke" the name of Jesus (Acts 9:14, 21; 26:10-12). After Saul became a Christian, they turned their fury on him and committed themselves to bringing about his death (Acts 22:30; 23:14; 25:15). As a class, they held tenaciously to their resurrection-denying theology and publicly opposed the church; but, amazingly, Luke reports that "a great many of the priests became obedient to the faith" (Acts 6:7).

In summary, then, the Jewish leaders as a group see Jesus as a threat to their status as teachers of the ways of God and to their influence among the people; according to them, he acts without authority and teaches a heretical theology. He must be stopped at all costs!

The Evaluations of Various Named Individuals

Most people in Luke's Gospel speak under the cloak of anonymity; only about a dozen people are named. Of those named individuals whose opinions about Jesus are given, only Judas Iscariot (obviously he saw Jesus as one deserving betrayal —Luke 22:3, 33), and Simon the Pharisee express negative evaluations (Luke 7:39).

John the baptizer saw Jesus as an apocalyptic figure who was mightier than himself (Luke 3:16-17). Although he would later raise the question as to whether Jesus was the "coming one", Luke seems to imply that Jesus' response was sufficient to remove the doubt (Luke 7:18-23).

Peter began following Jesus early and quickly developed a trust that would prompt him to fish in a hopeless situation because Jesus "said so" (Luke 5:5). When Jesus filled Peter's boat with fish to the point of sinking, Peter "fell down at Jesus' knees, saying, `Go away from me, Lord, for I am a sinful man'" (Luke 5:8) —a reaction reminiscent of Isaiah's when he saw the Lord "sitting on a throne, high and lofty"(Isaiah 6:5). Although not completely understanding it all, Peter apparently began at that moment to view Jesus as a person through whom he encountered the presence of deity. That was enough to cause him to leave "everything and follow" Jesus (Luke 5:11; 18:28). When asked by Jesus "who do you say that I am?" Peter affirms: "the Messiah of God" (Luke 9:20). While seeing apparitions of Moses and Elijah conversing with Jesus, Peter exclaims, "Master, it is good for us to be here; let us make three dwellings, one for you, one for Moses, and one for Elijah" (Luke 9:33). Although he did "not [know] what he said" he obviously saw Jesus as one who deserved at least the same honor as (if not more than) Moses (the greatest leader of his ancestors) and Elijah (arguably one of the most venerated of the ancient prophets). Although through fleshly weakness he thrice denied knowing Jesus (Luke 22:54-62), we find it easy to believe him when he says "Lord, I am ready to go with you to prison and death" (Luke 22:33). After his restoration, Peter consistently preaches that Jesus is: the one whom God raised from the dead; the one to whom David referred in his writings as "Lord"; God's "Holy One"; the resurrected "Messiah"; the one whom God "raised up" and "exalted at the right hand of God"; the "Lord and Messiah; and the only one in whose name there is salvation (Acts 2:22-36; 4:12).

Though we don't hear his actual voice, a tax collector named Levi spoke with eloquent actions when he left everything to follow Jesus (Luke 5:27). The same is true of the women Mary Magdalene, Joanna, and Susanna. So sure were they of his identity (likely seeing him as the Messiah) and so complete was their devotion that they followed Jesus from Galilee and provided him with financial support (Luke 8:2). Even after he was publicly humiliated and crucified, they remained loyal and made provisions to anoint his body for a proper burial (Luke 23:55-56; 24:8).

Mary and Martha invite Jesus into their home and while Martha breaks her back to provide the meal, Mary hangs on Jesus' every word — apparently taking the unlikely position as a disciple, which was scandalous for a woman in that patriarchal community. Martha, who was doing what was culturally expected (cooking and cleaning), complains to Jesus, "Lord, do you not care that my sister has left me to do all the work by myself? Tell her to help me" (Luke 10:40). Jesus' response is somewhat startling. "Martha, Martha, you are worried and distracted by many things; there is need of only one thing. Mary has chosen the better part, which will not be taken away from her" (Luke 10:41-42). Although Martha honors Jesus by her service, Luke seems to be saying that, in reality, Mary is modeling behavior that shows him even greater honor. After all, he had said: "My mother and my brothers are those who hear the word of God and do it" (Luke 8:21).

On one occasion, as Jesus was passing through the city of Jericho, a crowd pressed in on him. Zacchaeus, a tax collector who was rich in monetary wealth but diminutive in stature ran ahead and climbed a tree to gain an unobstructed view. When Jesus came to the point of passing beneath the tree he called Zacchaeus down announcing his desire to visit his house (Luke 19:1-5). In spite of the crowd's negative evaluation of him, Zacchaeus was so moved by Jesus' acceptance of him that he promised, "Look, half of my possessions, Lord, I will give to the poor; and if I have defrauded anyone of anything, I will pay back four times as much" (Luke 19:8). Jesus then announced: "Today salvation has come to this house, because he too is a son of Abraham. For the Son of Man has come to seek out and save the lost" (Luke 19:9-10). Luke likely presents this story as an example of how his readers should seek a clear understanding of Jesus and respond to his offer of salvation by a completely reformed life.

In spite of reports that Jesus' tomb is empty and that angels are announcing his resurrection, two disciples leave Jerusalem for their hometown of Emmaus, apparently hanging up their discipleship. In their downcast and hopeless state, they verbally mull over the events that had caused their discouragement. As they thus journey, surprisingly, Jesus joins them. Mysteriously, they are unable to recognize him and nonchalantly accept him into their company. He inquires about their discussion and one of them, Cleopas, responds with apparent irritation: "Are you the only stranger in Jerusalem who does not know the things that have taken place there in these days?" (Luke 24:18). In his opinion, Jesus was so significant that no one, not even one of the estimated 300,000 strangers who were in Jerusalem for the Passover could have been unaware of what had happened to him. Jesus asked, "What things?" To this feigned ignorance, the two disciples replied:

> The things about Jesus of Nazareth, who was a prophet mighty in deed and word before God and all the people, and how our chief priests and leaders handed him over to be condemned to death and crucified him. But we had hoped that he was the one to redeem Israel. Yes, and besides all this, it is now the third day since these things took place. Moreover, some women of our group astounded us. They were at the tomb early this morning, and when they did not find his body there, they came back and told us that they had indeed seen a vision of angels who said he was alive. Some of those who were with us went to the tomb and found it just as the women had said; but they did not see him. (Luke 24:19-24)

From the standpoint of Christian confession, the only thing this lacks is faith. In these words, the two from Emmaus foreshadow gospel preaching in all significant points: a human Jesus who was powerful in words and deeds was condemned to death and yet reported to be alive three days later. Had they believed the testimony they had heard, they would have realized that the redemption they had "hoped" he would bring was available (compare this with Acts 2:22-42 et al.). Of course, they did come to recognize him in the breaking of bread and rejoice (Luke 24:31-35)!

The Evaluations of Various Unnamed People

Most evaluations of Jesus come from unnamed individuals and crowds in Luke. Although representing the gamut of diverse opinions, there are a few broad generalizations that can be made. For example, the people in Nazareth have difficulty seeing beyond his family's ties to their community, to them he is simply a homeboy —the proverbial "prophet without honor" (see Luke 4:22-29). The people of Capernaum, however, see him as a prophet who deserves honor and is widely sought after (see Luke 4:32-40). This is the prevailing opinion of the masses throughout Galilee; he is pursued by many for his teachings and healings (Luke 5:1; 15, 19-26, et al.).

At times, many were willing to travel with him (Luke 14:25). Two other groups of people reject him unequivocally —the Gerasenes who had witnessed an exorcism that resulted in the destruction of a herd of swine (Luke 8:37) and a village of Samaritans who couldn't look past their petty prejudices against the Jews (Luke 9:51-56).

The crowds in Jerusalem run hot and cold. They welcome him with great adulation (Luke 19:36-38), are spellbound by his teaching (Luke 19:48), rise early to hear him teach in the temple (21:38), and yet call for his crucifixion (Luke 23:13-24), and watch in silence as he dies on the cross (23:35); they leave the scene of his death beating their breasts —apparently feeling remorse over the death of a fellow-Israelite, but missing it's significance (Luke 23:48).

One group that is almost constantly present throughout the story is the disciples. Although Jesus opens himself up to free and constant interaction with crowds and eats without discrimination with all, it is primarily on the disciples that he devotes his time and teaching (see especially Luke 6:17-49; 12:1; 12:22; 14:26-33; 16:1; et al.). From time to time we hear from one or more of them: "his disciples asked him what this parable meant" (Luke 8:9); "Master, Master, we are perishing" (Luke 8:24); "Lord, teach us to pray, as John taught his disciples to pray" (Luke 11:1); and, "Lord, should we strike with the sword?" (Luke 22:49).

Although they represent people of faith, their faith is never (within the story) perfected. Perhaps they are intended to serve as an identification point for Luke's readers; in other words, the disciples' experience of tenuous, yet growing, faith is paradigmatic for the readers.

Out of an unspecified, yet no doubt large, number of disciples, Jesus appointed twelve to be apostles (Luke 6:13) —that is "sent ones." On rare occasion, individual apostles (such as Peter, John, and James) are given speaking roles (Luke 5:5; 9:33; 9:49; 9:54), but for the most part they are represented as a group. And, as a collective they are credited with only a few statements of direct address: "Increase our faith" (Luke 17:5); "Send the crowd away, so that they may go into the surrounding villages and countryside, to lodge and get provisions; for we are here in a deserted place" (Luke 9:12); "We have no more than five loaves and two fish — unless we are to go and buy food for all these people" (Luke 9:13); "Lord, look, here are two swords" (Luke 22:38); and, "The Lord has risen indeed, and he has appeared to Simon!" (Luke 24:34). Prior to their acceptance of the resurrection they are inconsistent in their understanding of his identity. In the Acts, though, their faith is settled and secure; they consistently proclaim without fail that Jesus is the risen Savior (Acts 2:1-42; 4:33; 5:29; et al.).

Jesus' Evaluation of Himself

In Luke, Jesus is portrayed as having a solid understanding of himself. While we might reasonably suppose that he grew in that understanding, and gradually came to know his identity and purpose through the things he learned and experienced (see for instance Hebrews 5:8), the Gospel of Luke shows none of that. In fact, aside from one rather ambiguous scene from his childhood in which he claimed it was obvious that his parents should have expected to find him "in [his] Father's house" (Luke 2:49), Jesus is presented as having a clear understanding of his identity and as one who acted and spoke consistent with it.[29] He claims to fulfill the Messianic prophecies (Luke 4:21; 7:22; 18:31-33; 22:37; 24:25-27; 24:46-47), often refers to himself with the Messianic title "Son of Man" (Luke 6:5; 7:34; 9:22; et al).), and claims to have the authority to call for obedience and sacrifice (Luke 6:47-49; 9:2318:29-30; et al.).

From the time his inner circle of apostles is able to confess him as the Messiah, he demonstrates a knowledge of his fate: "The Son of Man must undergo great suffering, and be rejected by the elders, chief priests, and scribes, and be killed, and on the third day be raised" (Luke 9:22, et al.). He is "greater than Solomon" and "greater than Jonah" (Luke 11:31-32). He has the authority to forgive sin (Luke 5:24), to confer the kingdom of

God (Luke 22:28-30), and would —as the Son of God —be exalted to the highest place in heaven (Luke 22:67).

He sees himself as having been sent with a message (Luke 10:16) and as one who speaks with authority about the kingdom of God (Luke 18:16). He even claimed knowledge of such other-worldly events as Satan's fall from heaven and his request for the ability to tempt the apostles (Luke 10:18; 22:31). In Luke, Jesus expresses no doubt as to why he has come: "the Son of Man came to seek out and to save the lost" (Luke 19:10).

Discipleship: Christology Meets Christopraxis

Lukan Christology has practical implications for those who would follow Jesus —it has an implied christopraxis. The gravity of discipleship is taken very seriously in Luke-Acts. At one point, it almost seems as though Jesus was trying to talk people out of discipleship:

> Whoever comes to me and does not hate father and mother, wife and children, brothers and sisters, yes, and even life itself, cannot be my disciple. Whoever does not carry the cross and follow me cannot be my disciple.
>
> . . .
>
> So therefore, none of you can become my disciple if you do not give up all your possessions. (Luke 14:26-33)

Obviously, following Jesus is a serious matter. So what does it mean to be a disciple of Jesus? Dallas Willard has insightfully described discipleship with the word "apprenticeship." An "apprentice is simply someone who has decided to be with another person, under appropriate conditions, in order to become capable of what that person does or to become what that person is" (282). What is it that Jesus does? He "lives in the kingdom of God, and he applies that kingdom for the good of others and even makes it possible for them to enter it for themselves" (282-283). A disciple is one who says, then, "I am learning from Jesus to live my life as he would if he were I" (283).

It is this kind of apprenticeship that we see demonstrated in Luke. The main contours of Jesus' public life are re-echoed in the actions of his disciples. Just like their Master they are accused of eating with "tax collectors and sinners" (Luke 5:30 see 15:2), and of doing "what is not lawful on the Sabbath" (Luke 6:2 see 13:14-16). He empowered them to cast out demons and to cure the sick —both key aspects of his ministry (Luke 9:1 see 8:2). While they do enjoy some success in that ministry, they fail on one occasion, reminding us that they have not yet perfected their discipleship (Luke 9:42). On another occasion, he charged them with the task of feeding a huge crowd —a feat the reader surmises only Jesus can accomplish. When they obeyed his simple commands, though, they were able to feed the crowd with the abundant resources he provided (Luke 9:13-16).

Jesus speaks with authority about the kingdom of God. He goes about "proclaiming and bringing the good news of the kingdom of God" (Luke 8:1). To the disciples, he said "To you it has been given to know the secrets of the kingdom of God" (Luke 8:9); and "he sent them out to proclaim the kingdom of God" (Luke 9:2). It is precisely being like Jesus that the disciples are about in the Luke-Acts. Although doing it imperfectly, it is obvious that they are seeking to "be fully qualified" and thus "like [their] teacher" (Luke 6:40). Learning from Jesus how to be an effective disciple is one of the most important reasons to read Luke-Acts. Being a more authentic disciple is another way of describing the goal of identity-reshaping that occupies this project

Summary and Trajectory

Luke's story of Jesus brings together a number of diverse and, at times, contradictory evaluations of Jesus' identity. It is obvious that the author intends certain points of view to be seen as consonant with his own (such as the supernatural evaluations, and Jesus' own evaluations); but he also expects the reader to recognize some perspectives as patently spurious (such as the chief priests' who believed he was worthy of death). Mainly, though, it seems that the evangelist desires the reader to relate to various individuals at their diverse stages of faith, and to grow, through the narrative encounters this Gospel makes possible, to an understanding of Jesus as universal savior —the savior he or she needs.

This concludes the research section of this project. The chapters to follow present a specific application of the research. The project described in Chapter 5 is the outline of a proposed adult class study on the topic "Reshaping Christian Identity." This study will offer a context for a person whose Christian identity has been inadequately based in doctrinal or institutional distinctiveness to allow that identity to be reshaped christologically. As was concluded in chapter 2, Christology should not be shaped by prevailing philosophies (hence, devising a Christ after one's own likeness); Christology should, instead, move in the other direction — toward allowing the person of Jesus whom one meets in the Gospels to shape the inquirer. Chapter 3 underscored the significance of narrative by suggesting that it is both normative for human experience and the dominant genre through which the Gospels convey christological data.

The Gospel is, after all, a story. As such, it has the power to shape identity.

This chapter has explored the identity of Jesus as it is presented in Luke-Acts. Although this chapter has tended to distill the individual perspectives from the Lukan narrative framework, it is the narrative scenes themselves that give these perspectives context and meaning. In other words, it is within the narrative scenarios that we understand why some viewpoints are valid and others are invalid. And it is in these scenarios that discipleship is made real. The challenge of the project's proposal will be to select narrative scenes from Luke-Acts that will effectively serve as catalysts for the reshaping of Christian identity.

CHAPTER 5

THE IMPLICATIONS FOR MINISTRY

Introduction

When I prepared the initial proposal for this project/dissertation, I listed three implications that the proposed study held for my ministry and me:

1. Since I have long held an inadequate basis for my Christian identity, I need to reshape that identity christologically;
2. My writing and speaking need to be reexamined and readjusted so that I no longer reinforce the Church of Christ's inadequate method of reckoning Christian identity (i.e., doctrinally); and,
3. My awareness of the problem and its surmised solution implies the need for me to intentionally direct more of my ministerial energies (i.e., written and spoken) toward helping others reshape their identities.

Since embarking on this study I have experienced some dramatic changes in my life and ministry. I began the project while in my seventh year working as a writer and lecturer with a parachurch organization that produces Christian Evidences literature for the Church of Christ. A year into my study, I found myself laboring under a cloud of increasing suspicion and doubt regarding my doctrinal soundness. In response, I returned to pastoral ministry, accepting the call to a church in Peachtree City, Georgia (January 1997). After only eight months, the congregation split and I resigned. Presently, I am serving as Senior Minister of the Church of Christ in Bellevue, Washington (since April, 1998). The first job change was precipitated by both my loss of confidence in an identity that is centered around doctrinal distinctives, which my work virtually required me to propagate, and by my coworkers' resulting loss of confidence in me for doubting the validly of such a center. The split in the Georgian church was driven by a handful of powerful people who believed I was not "faithful" because I was unwilling to denounce certain progressive thinkers in the Church of Christ. My unwillingness to "mark" such men and women as false teachers was a sign to them that I no longer held to the Church of Christ's distinctive doctrines. This belief raised doubts about the direction the church was heading with me in leadership. This criticism of me and their unwillingness to allow the church to shift its center of identity away from doctrine drove those members who felt otherwise to leave the congregation (more than half). At that point I felt the potential for positive ministry had been completely undermined, and saw no option but to resign.

A few months later I began ministering to a church that has been moving away from its doctrinal center for awhile, but has not had a clear understanding of what should be at the center. In the year-and-a-half since moving to Bellevue, I have been attempting to make Christology central and to develop a christocentric basis for ministry.

The upheaval of the past three years has strengthened my conviction that the Church of Christ is indeed in the throes of an identity crisis and that this project's proposed solution is very promising. I have made significant progress in shifting the center of my own identity away from the church's doctrinal distinctives and toward my relationship with Jesus Christ. I have been preaching more christocentric sermons and have been teaching classes on the role of Christology in discipleship. My original implications have certainly directed my ministry. Now that I have studied in greater depth the three pillars upon which my project stands (Christology, narrative theology, and the identity of Jesus in Luke-Acts), I recognize a whole new set of implications for ministry.

Implications from my study of Christology

My study of Christology has made me more aware of the broad diversity of opinions regarding the identity of Jesus Christ. As I considered the various views, both ancient and contemporary, I concluded that christological inquiry, generally, starts from one of two different beginning points and influences, ultimately, the question of Christian identity. It either starts from an understanding of what it means to be human (and with preconceived notions about Jesus' humanity), or from the testimony of Scripture regarding the identity of Jesus. From either starting point, consideration is then given to how the identity of Jesus influences the identity of those who follow him (i.e., "In light of who Jesus is, who am I?").

If, on the one hand, I view Jesus as a cynic sage (a view based on the preconceived notions of the Fellows of the Jesus Seminar), then my identity as a Christian will, in turn, likely take on the appearance of a social critic who stands on the sociological sidewalk issuing pithy critiques of conventional religious wisdom and practices. On the other hand, if beginning with the Scriptures I come to view Jesus as the "cosmic Christ" (as did Jürgen Moltmann), my identity as a Christian likely will include an awareness of my having been created for fellowship with deity and for participation in the redemption of the entire cosmos.

The first implication for ministry that this study provides is a warning: be sure the Christ you follow is not the Christ you create. Christology is always in danger of being unduly influenced by the pull of cultural tides and it is entirely possible for one to find oneself embracing a counterfeit. This is as true today in our "politically correct" age as it was in the age of second-century gnosticism, or nineteenth-century liberalism.

The second implication is that as a preacher of the Gospel, I need to be sure to present the Christ in all his strangeness and ambiguities. I realized along the way that for much of my ministry I have been preaching a rather benign —mostly warm and friendly —Jesus who didn't really challenge my lifestyle or thought-patterns. The Jesus I preached seemed simply to smile and urge his followers to be nice and avoid immoral behavior. My study of Christology has revealed a different Jesus —one who associated with the "wrong" people, criticized the "right" people, and put his obedience to God above all personal convenience. I met a Jesus whom, I now believe, is only accurately preached when regularly I feel uncomfortable in his company and stung by his teaching. At the same time, though, I see in him an authentic humanness and inexplicable deity for which I deeply yearn.

Implications from my study of narrative theology

Narrative theology was crucial to this study because of the insights it offers relative to the shaping of personal identity and the way the gospel, as story, impacts our lives. We are, after all, story beings living in a story world who are guided by the stories of Scripture. The gospel narratives provide opportunity for men and women to experience a collision of their personal identities (the stories of who they are) with the identity of Jesus Christ; ideally, the byproduct of such an encounter is "conversion" (a reshaping of identity). As my personal story collides with the story of Jesus ("collision" is used intentionally here to underscore the fact that —heard properly —the story of Jesus is radical and jarring rather than comfortable and easily domesticated by contemporary people compromised, as we are, by sin), I have the opportunity to reinterpret my understanding of the world and my place within it. This narrative encounter (collision), then, provides me an occasion to be changed.

One implication that arises out of my study of narrative is that I need ever to be cognizant of the story of which I am a part. My story is constantly being updated. Through my actual empirical experiences, and those gained through narratives, I am being changed. Those changes can move me closer to, or further from, faithful discipleship. This being true, I need to consciously avoid participation in ungodly, kingdom of God-denying stories. As Paul put it, "bad company ruins good morals" (1 Corinthians 15:33). My "conversion" is never totally complete.

A second —and related —implication of the study of narrative is that I need to continually return to, and re-experience the Scripture's stories of Jesus. In this way, I am able to relive the actions and better understand the intentions of my teacher. As a Christian, I want my story to be one of a disciple who is becoming more like my teacher (Luke 6:40); this won't happen by accident. This will require an ongoing conversation with the biblical stories of Jesus.

A third implication is that I need to improve my story-telling skills. If the "power of God for salvation" is the "gospel" (Romans 1:16), then it stands to reason that my ability to tell that story will either help or hinder the story's impact on other people. The truth is, people love a good story and the gospel of Jesus Christ is the greatest story ever told. As such, it deserves to be told with the very best skill.

Implications from my study of the identity of Jesus in Luke-Acts

Luke-Acts provided the specific textual environment for the project. As an example of narrative theology, Luke-Acts enables us to encounter Jesus in an identity-shaping way. Luke-Acts presents us with a portrait of Jesus as universal savior whose ministry of seeking after and saving the lost was intended to benefit each of us, and to challenge every distortion of humanity that sin has caused (e.g., dysfunctional human relationships, self-destructive behavior, and separation from fellowship with the Creator). Regardless of where we are spiritually when we meet Luke's Jesus, we confront both judgment and grace —judgment for the ways that we fail to live up to our design as sons and daughters of God, and grace in the knowledge that we are accepted as we are and given the power to be transformed completely. Whether libertarian or legalistic, we all can be saved.

My study of the identity of Jesus in Luke-Acts implies that as a disciple of Jesus, I am invited to participate in the Messianic mission described by Isaiah and repeated by Jesus:

> The Spirit of the Lord is upon me, because he has anointed me to bring good news to the poor. He has sent me to proclaim release to the captives and recovery of sight to the blind, to let the oppressed go free, to proclaim the year of the Lord's favor. (Luke 4:18-19)

My preaching and living needs to both dispute the world's values and embody the values of the Kingdom of God. Although perhaps conveyed through different specific cultural expressions, the community of middle-class Euro-Americans to whom I minister are as compromised by fleshly values as were the people to whom Jesus first spoke those words. I know this to be true because I myself strive to have more and more material wealth and act as though the more one has, the more important one is. I also categorize people based on stereotypes and withhold my company from people who are in groups that are different from mine. I still hold grudges, still struggle with forgiving those who wrong me, and am still slow to seek the forgiveness of those I wrong. The Messiah's agenda, though, requires me to look beyond myself and to see where the message of Jubilee ("the year of the Lord's favor") needs to be heard and felt and to be there with good news for the poor, captive, blind and oppressed.

Another implication from my study of the identity of Jesus in Luke-Acts is that today, as in Luke's day, people are at various levels of understanding about who Jesus is. Some saw Jesus as little more than a good teacher, others saw him as a prophet of God, an exorcist, or a miracle-worker. Some were perceptive enough to see that Jesus was fulfilling God's will and that his ministry was in some way related to the coming of the kingdom of God (Luke 19:11). All these evaluations were valid, but inadequate. Every age has its share of articulate communicators, women and men capable of amazing accomplishments, and those through whom God works to promote the kingdom agenda. But Luke's narrative pushes us to see that Jesus is more than that. Jesus is the Savior who brings hope to the world and at whose feet God is praised (Luke 2:11; 17:15-16). Sharing these stories brings clarity where there is confusion and facilitates personal encounters with Jesus that encourage and enhance discipleship.

Many in the Christian community are like the two people mentioned by Luke who claimed they would follow Jesus but needed first to take care of personal business (Luke 9:57-62). Intellectually, they know that discipleship means leaving everything and following Jesus (Luke 5:11), but they are holding back. Hearing the Lukan narratives in contemporary terms offers opportunities for them to enter into ever-increasing levels of commitment.

Summary and Trajectory

All of these implications really support a simple conviction. The more we as individuals and as a denomination set our eyes on Jesus, the greater spiritual vitality we will experience. I believe that when each member of the church understands herself or himself primarily as a disciple of Jesus and secondarily as a member of the Church of Christ, we will begin, as a group, to enjoy stronger unity, and offer a more convincing witness to the world of the presence of the Kingdom of God. In my view, Narrative Christology offers the most exciting opportunity to see that kind of change occur.

CHAPTER 6
A PROPOSED ACT OF MINISTRY

Introduction

I have concluded from my experiences as both a member and as a minister that the Church of Christ (individually and collectively) is experiencing an identity crisis. In the Church of Christ, Christian identity is commonly reckoned according to an inadequate point of reference: doctrinal and institutional distinctiveness. In other words, members usually understand and describe who they are as Christians (their Christian identity) by reciting the Church of Christ's distinctive doctrines (that is, the doctrines that distinguish it from other groups that claim Christian allegiance) and/or by reciting their understanding of the Church of Christ's institutional identity (that is, its interpretation of church history and the ordinances it observes).

Inadequacies of the Current Method

I contend that this method of reckoning identity is inadequate for at least four reasons. First, it short-changes the grace of God and fosters a system of justification by works. This is so because it locates a person's right-standing with God in her or his ability to understand and articulate the church's doctrinal platform and in the performance of the church's ordinances rather than in the finished work of Jesus on the cross and her or his acceptance of salvation as an undeserved gift.

Second, this method of reckoning Christian identity is powerless to bring about the true conversion intended by Jesus Christ. In fact, hardly any conversion is necessary if Christianity is simply a body of doctrine. Unregenerate souls can believe (give mental assent to), teach, and defend most any doctrine without first being changed by it. Example after example could be cited of churches being split in the name of "unity." Not a few powerful pulpiteers have lived sexually twisted lives for years without detection; they said the "right" things so no one questioned their morality. Countless is the number of Christians who live spiritually anemic, stagnant lives all the while able to defend the "truth" and spot a "false teacher" the proverbial mile away.

Third, it tends to be divisive. If my Christian identity is wrapped up in doctrinal distinctives, then all who do not hold those doctrines with the same level of conviction, or communicate them with the same terminology as I do are suspect, at best. At worst, they are heretical and I should not have fellowship with them. If several people in my congregation change in their understanding of a given doctrinal issue that was settled decades earlier (such as whether the Holy Spirit indwells a believer, or whether women may audibly pray in the presence of men), then the climate is set for a church split. If doctrinal unanimity is the glue holding a community together, then any divergence of opinion shatters the fellowship.

Fourth, from a pragmatic standpoint, this method of reckoning Christian identity is inadequate because members of the Church of Christ seem increasingly less concerned about the church's distinctiveness and more concerned about having personal faith that is relevant to the challenges of contemporary life. In what some have termed our "post-Christian" world, denominational loyalties can be no longer taken for granted and churches that focus on doctrinal distinctives are seen as irrelevant to a great number of spiritual travelers. In the marketplace, churches that appear to offer only "right" doctrine are bypassed in favor of those that offer participation in a relational community.

This is a crucial area of concern because a Christian who has an inadequate or confused identity is incapable of bearing a faithful witness of Christ to the world and of finding the power to live the faith he or she professes. This project proposes to help members of the Church of Christ reshape their Christian identity.

Research Issues

It is my belief that a better way of reckoning Christian identity is according to one's encounter with, understanding of, and relationship to, Jesus Christ. Hence, this project stands on a synthesis of three areas of research: Christology; narrative theology; and Luke-Acts. Since I am proposing that Christian identity should be shaped christologically, a basic understanding of how the church historically has struggled to understand the identity of Jesus Christ was essential. I found that christological inquiry, generally, starts from one of two different beginning points and influences, ultimately, the question of Christian identity. It either starts from an understanding of what it means to be human (and with preconceived notions about Jesus' humanity), or from the testimony of Scripture regarding the identity of Jesus. From either starting point, consideration is then given to how the identity of Jesus influences the identity of those who follow him (i.e., "In light of who Jesus is, who am I?"). If, on the one hand, I view Jesus as a cynic sage (a view based on the preconceived notions of the Fellows of the Jesus Seminar), then my identity as a Christian will, in turn, likely take on the appearance of a social critic who stands on the sociological sidewalk issuing pithy critiques of conventional religious wisdom and practices. On the other hand, if beginning with the Scriptures I come to view Jesus as the "cosmic Christ" (as did Jürgen Moltmann), my identity as a Christian likely will include an awareness of my having been created for fellowship with deity and for participation in the redemption of the entire cosmos.

Narrative theology was crucial to this study because of the insights it offers relative to the shaping of personal identity and the way the gospel, as story, impacts our lives. We are, after all, story beings living in a story world who are guided by the stories of Scripture. The gospel narratives provide opportunity for men and women to experience a collision of their personal identities (the stories of who they are) with the identity of Jesus Christ; ideally, the byproduct of such an encounter is "conversion" (a reshaping of identity). As my personal story collides with the story of Jesus ("collision" is used intentionally here to underscore the fact that —heard properly —the story of Jesus is radical and jarring rather than comfortable and easily domesticated by contemporary people compromised, as we are, by sin), I have the opportunity to reinterpret my understanding of the world and my place within it. This narrative encounter (collision), then, provides me an occasion to be changed.

Luke-Acts provided the specific textual environment for the project. As an example of narrative theology, Luke-Acts enables us to encounter Jesus in an identity-shaping way. Luke-Acts presents us with a portrait of Jesus as universal savior whose ministry of seeking after and saving the lost was intended to benefit each of us, and to challenge every distortion of humanity that sin has caused (e.g., dysfunctional human relationships, self-destructive behavior, and separation from fellowship with the Creator). Regardless of where we are spiritually when we meet Luke's Jesus, we confront both judgment and grace —judgment for the ways that we fail to live up to our design as sons and daughters of God, and grace in the knowledge that we are accepted as we are and given the power to be transformed completely. Whether libertarian or legalistic, we all can be saved.

The Proposed Act of Ministry

The Act of Ministry that I am proposing is the writing of a study guide-type adult class book on the subject of reshaping Christian identity christologically.

The General Plan of the Study Guide

This book is designed to be used by members of the Church of Christ who are beginning to sense (or who have long felt) an emptiness in their spiritual lives and are dissatisfied with the option of ignoring it and going on as though it doesn't matter. The study guide will consist of eight chapters plus a prologue and an epilogue. Although it can be used for individual study, primarily it is intended for use by adult Sunday school classes or small group studies. The reason for this is that to be a Christian is to be a participant in a community of faith and the inter-action of other believers will multiply the benefit of the discussion periods. Each chapter will contain discussion questions so that immediate, practical application can be made of material that is being studied.

Objectives of the Study Guide

The primary goal of the study guide is to encourage a reshaping of Christian identity. While it would be too ambitious to expect a single study guide to effectively lead every student/group to a completely reshaped identity, it is conceivable that a study guide could put people on a pathway toward such reshaping. Achieving this goal will entail the accomplishment of a few smaller and more specific objectives. First, the study guide should assist the students/group in articulating an understanding of the identity of Luke's Jesus and of the meaning of salvation in Luke-Acts. Second, the study guide should aid the students/group to be able to describe in practical terms what it means for the contemporary church to continue the ministry Jesus announced in Luke 4:18-19. Third, the study guide should help the students/group better understand the meaning of personal identity (the general factors that shape it, its susceptibility to unwanted influence and its vulnerability to self-deception). Fourth, the study guide should provide an opportunity for the students/group to experience (and reflect upon) the collision between their personal stories and the identity of Jesus as he is presented in representative Lukan narratives.

Brief Explanation of Each Chapter

Prologue: An Identity Crisis

The prologue will consist of a brief, realistic, and disturbing narrative describing the feelings of hopelessness and frustration experienced by a Christian whose identity has been based upon the inadequate foundation of doctrinal and institutional distinctives. The prologue will simply name the problem, but not offer any resolution.

Chapter 1: The Mis-Shaping of Christian Identity

Recalling the Enlightenment roots and polemical path followed by the Church of Christ for much of the past 150 years, this chapter will explore some of the causes of the present identity crisis and consider the role narrative plays in the shaping of personal identity. Obvious symptoms of the crisis (such as the fact that the church has emphasized doctrine over relationships and exclusivity over unity) will be discussed as will our vulnerability to self-delusion. The discussion questions will center on the students'/group's awareness of the crisis and the devastating consequences such crisis brings to the health of the church and the effectiveness of its witness for Christ and participation in Christ's ongoing ministry.

Chapter 2: What Are They Saying about Jesus?

As in the days of Jesus' earthly sojourn, the air is filled with contradictory and sometimes blasphemous opinions about the identity of Jesus. Using the first of two questions Jesus asked his disciples ("Who do the crowds say that I am?" Luke 9:18) as a starting point, this chapter will discuss in brief the wide diversity of opinions about the identity of Jesus prevalent in contemporary society. This will underscore the need for a scriptural basis for understanding Jesus' identity. The discussion questions will focus on the possible sources/motives for such diversity and on the practical implication these inadequate christologies have for Christian identity.

Chapter 3: Who Do You Say Jesus Is?

Using the second of the two questions Jesus asked his disciples ("But who do you say that I am?" Luke 9:20) as a starting point, this chapter will discuss Peter's response ("the Messiah of God" Luke 9:20) and its implications regarding Jesus' identity. Narrative clues to Jesus' identity as Messiah will be ferreted out of the Lukan gospel. What led Peter to make this amazing confession? Questions for group discussion will center on two issues. First, how does the student/group understand the identity of Jesus and how does that understanding fit with the meaning of Messiahship? Second, what implications for discipleship does Messiah imply?

Chapter 4: Meeting Jesus in Luke, Encounter 1

This chapter will begin with a retelling of the story of Jesus' return to his hometown synagogue and how it almost cost him his life (Luke 4:14-30). This story juxtaposes the favorable reception of Jesus in Galilee with the unfavorable response to his message in Nazareth. The meaning of salvation and the purposes of God are defined in this story and rejected by those who might reasonably be most likely to embrace them. The discussion questions will lead the students/group to explore the grace and judgment of God's purposes and this story. Where does one find oneself in the narrative? If in the place of the Galileans, what might cause one to identify with the Nazarenes? If in the place of the Nazarenes, what might cause one to identify with the Galileans? From the issue of identification, the students/ group will be led to contemplate how the contemporary church might perceive its role in continuing the mission inauger-ated by Jesus in this story?

Chapter 5: Meeting Jesus in Luke, Encounter 2

This chapter will begin with a retelling of the story of Jesus' Sabbath-day meal with a leader of the Pharisees (Luke 14:1-24). This multifaceted story is a classic Lukan portrayal of Jesus. It shows him in conflict with the Pharisees, contains controversy over appropriate Sabbath-day behavior, exploits the prevailing customs governing honor and shame as demonstrated in table fellowship, and contrasts the priorities of God with the misplaced priorities of fallen humanity. The discussion questions will address the matter of how one encounters the priorities of God in Jesus' example and teaching. They will seek to bring to the surface the identifications the students/group make when hearing the story and challenge students/group to hear the judgment and grace Jesus is explicating in this setting.

Chapter 6: Meeting Jesus in Luke, Encounter 3

This chapter will begin by retelling the story of Jesus' journey to Emmaus with two disciples on the brink of despair (Luke 24:13-35). In this story, Jesus is present from almost the beginning to almost the end and is its central character. By playing the role of an uninformed stranger (since his disciples do not recognize him), Jesus is put in the peculiar position of being able to hear his own story told from the perspective of those who have lost their faith in him. But this is just the beginning, since the story ends with these same disciples excitedly spreading the good news of Jesus' resurrection. The discussion questions will aim at encouraging identification with the disciples and explore the transformation that occurs between their faithless report of the resurrection testimonies and their own faith-full report of the same.

Chapter 7: The Transformation of Simon Peter

This chapter will pair two Lukan narratives that demonstrate the change Jesus brought to Simon Peter's life (Luke 22:31-34, 54-62 and Acts 4:1-22). This pairing will be accomplished by using the Acts 4 narrative as the primary text with flashbacks to the Luke 22 narrative. The emphasis will be upon the Christology at the core of the transformation of Peter —who changed from being the disciple who denied knowing Jesus to the one who affirmed —in the face of persecution —"There is salvation in no one else [besides Jesus]" (Acts 4:12a). The discussion questions will encourage students to identify with Peter at his stage of denial and urge creative reflection regarding the impetus for the change that enabled Peter to defend what he had earlier denied. This opens the door to consider what is the salvation Jesus provides and what was its particular expression in Peter's life?

Chapter 8: The Transformation of Saul of Tarsus

This chapter will begin by telling of the story of how Saul of Tarsus encountered the risen Jesus and was completely changed by the experience (Acts 9:1-22). Discussion questions will center on possible preconceptions (and delusions) Saul may have held regarding the identity of Jesus, and how those preconceptions collapsed in the en-counter. What of the students'/group's personal stories can be challenged by this story and what does it say about discipleship?

Epilogue: The Hope of a Reshaped Identity

The epilogue will continue the narrative of the prologue and describe the difference an identity-shaping en-counter with Jesus can make. Hopelessness and spiritual anemia will be turned to hopefulness and excited participation in the ongoing ministry of Christ.

A Proposed Study Guide on Christian Identity

Evaluation Form

I. Please rate the following statements using this scale of judgment: 1 Strongly Agree, 2 Agree, 3 Undecided, 4 Disagree, 5 Strongly Disagree

_____ The description of the study guide is clearly stated.

_____ The study guide is well designed for its purpose.

_____ The goals and objectives of the study guide are clearly stated.

_____ The goals and objectives of the study guide are relevant for members of the Church of Christ.

______ The suggested chapters are consistent with the goals and objectives of the study guide.

______ The suggested chapters are sufficient for the purpose of the study guide.

______ The study guide shows promise in addressing the identity crisis experienced by many members of the Church of Christ.

II Please respond briefly to the following questions:

1. What are the strengths and weaknesses of the study guide as proposed?

2. How would you suggest improving the proposed study guide?

3. Speak briefly to the relevance of the proposed study guide both to members of the Church of Christ as well as to the larger Christian community:

4. Would you recommend such a study guide to a member of the Church of Christ? Why or why not?

5. Feel free to share other thoughts regarding the proposed study guide.

CHAPTER 7

EVALUATIONS OF THE PROPOSED ACT OF MINISTRY

Introduction

As a way to address the identity crisis that I believe holds the Church of Christ captive, I am proposing to write a study guide-type adult class book on the subject of reshaping Christian identity christologically. This is my "Proposed Act of Ministry" (see Chapter 6 of which the following is a summary).

This book will be designed to be used by members of the Church of Christ who are beginning to sense (or who have long felt) an emptiness in their spiritual lives and are dissatisfied with the option of ignoring it and going on as though it doesn't matter. The study guide will consist of eight chapters plus a prologue and an epilogue. Although it can be used for individual study, primarily it is intended for use by adult Sunday school classes or small group studies. The reason for this is that to be a Christian is to be a participant in a community of faith and the inter-action of other believers will multiply the benefit of the discussion periods. Each chapter will contain discussion questions so that immediate, practical application can be made of material that is being studied.

The primary goal of the study guide is to encourage a reshaping of Christian identity. While it would be too ambitious to expect a single study guide to effectively lead every student/group to a completely reshaped identity, it is conceivable that a study guide could put people on a pathway toward such reshaping.

Achieving this goal will entail the accomplishment of a few smaller and more specific objectives. First, the study guide should assist the students/group in articulating an understanding of the identity of Luke's Jesus and of the meaning of salvation in Luke-Acts. Second, the study guide should aid the students/group to be able to describe in practical terms what it means for the contemporary church to continue the ministry Jesus announced in Luke 4:18-19. Third, the study guide should help the students/group better understand the meaning of personal identity (the general factors that shape it, its susceptibility to unwanted influence and its vulnerability to self-deception). Fourth, the study guide should provide an opportunity for the students/group to experience (and reflect upon) the collision between their personal stories and the identity of Jesus as he is presented in representative Lukan narratives.

The Experts

In order to assess the potential for success that such a study guide might have, I prepared a brief document describing the proposed book (including the above goals and objectives and its planned chapters), and submitted it to four experts for evaluation (namely, Dr. John Mark Hicks, Mr. Wade Hodges, Dr. Milton Jones, and Dr. Floyd Parker). The experts were chosen because of their expertise in one or more areas of study. Dr. Hicks is Professor of Christian Doctrine at Harding University Graduate School of Religion (Memphis, Tennessee). He regularly teaches on the varieties of Theology and Christology. Dr. Hicks is also one of the founding ministers of a new church in Memphis, Tennessee that is intentionally targeting Generation X. Mr. Hodges is the preaching minister for the Sterling Drive Church of Christ (Bellingham, Washington). He is also a very gifted biblical storyteller. Dr. Jones is Professor of Homiletics and Evangelism at Puget Sound Christian College (Edmonds, Washington) where he teaches classes on various approaches to preaching and personal evangelism. He is also the minister of preaching for the Northwest Church of Christ (Shoreline, Washington), which has a strong ministry to students at the University of Washington. Dr. Parker is an Associate Professor of Bible at Faulkner University (Montgomery, Alabama) who teaches courses in New Testament and Christology. Each of these experts not only has a professional and academic background that makes their evaluations desirable, but each is also very concerned over the present crisis.

The Evaluations

The evaluation form was divided into two sections. In the first section the experts were asked to agree or disagree with seven positive statements about the proposal by assigning a number to indicate their judgment (1 = Strongly Agree; 2 = Agree; 3 = Undecided; 4 = Disagree; 5 = Strongly Disagree). In the second section the experts were asked to respond briefly to questions relating to the study guide. I will first give the experts' answers to the questionnaire and then comment on their specific responses.

The Experts' Answers to the Questions in Section One

1. The description of the study guide is clearly stated.

Hicks: 1; Hodges: 2; Jones: 1; Parker: 1

2. The study guide is well designed for its purpose.

Hicks: 1; Hodges: 2; Jones: 1; Parker: 1

3. The goals and objectives of the study guide are clearly stated.

Hicks: 1; Hodges: 1; Jones: 1; Parker: 1

4. The goals and objectives of the study guide are relevant for members of the Church of Christ.

Hicks: 1; Hodges: 2; Jones: 1; Parker: 1

5. The suggested chapters are consistent with the goals and objectives of the study guide.

Hicks: 1; Hodges: 2; Jones: 1; Parker: 1

6. The suggested chapters are sufficient for the purpose of the study guide.

Hicks: 2; Hodges: 2; Jones: 2; Parker: 1

7. The study guide shows promise in addressing the identity crisis experienced by many members of the Church of Christ.

Hicks: 2; Hodges: 1; Jones: 2; Parker: 1

The Experts' Answers to the Questions in Section Two

1. What are the strengths and weaknesses of the study guide as proposed?

- **Strengths:**

Dr. Hicks:

The strengths are root in narrative, the choice of texts in Luke-Acts, and the development of themes of personal transformation and encounter with Jesus.

Mr. Hodges:

The study guide will engage the group with powerful stories that should shake up their paradigms to some degree.

Dr. Jones:

The identity crisis in the Churches of Christ has been around for a long time but has escalated to the point that one wonders about the validity of the future of this movement. As identified, the Churches of Christ miss the identity of Jesus which is the key to their renewal. However, they seem to be blind to this problem and trying to solve the problem in another arena.

Dr. Parker:

The narrative element which you will be bringing to this study is of tremendous value for several reasons: 1) The narrative approach will teach the student to read scripture holistically, rather than mining scripture for proof texts to support traditional doctrinal belief (as has been done in the past). This alone is a step in the right direction; and, 2) I think that the idea of "living in a story world" will prove interesting and challenging for many members of the Church of Christ. As they learn to ask "what is Jesus doing in this story" or "what is God doing in the ministry of Jesus," they will also learn to ask "what is God doing in my story/ministry." I imagine that this will be a breath of fresh air for those who have been attempting to have a relationship with an institution for years.

- **Weaknesses:**

Dr. Hicks:

I think the weakness —which my "2s" above suggest —is that it does not appear to reshape the vision of the church as much as individual relationships. I see the communal emphasis (so this is not lacking), but what is perhaps lacking is a reflection on how this new vision of Jesus and this new identity is ecclesiologically connected. How can "Church of Christers" find their identity here and maintain their communal heritage (or is that a good goal)? How will this new vision of Jesus reshape their appropriated heritage in ways that they affirm their identity in Jesus but at the same time are not disconnected from their heritage in ways that would undermine the goal of the study itself (which is partly to maintain connection with their heritage, but to have a more biblical, christological, understanding of the church).

Mr. Hodges:

Is the real problem for church of Christers rooted in poor or undeveloped Christology or should it be traced back even farther to God the father? Much of Church of Christ theology was crystallized in fear of doing something wrong that would land us in hell (better safe than sorry theology). Doesn't this give us an image of God who is looking for reasons to send us to hell instead of pulling strings so that we can share eternity with him?

Dr. Jones:

I would love for this study guide to solve the problem. I have become skeptical of the people who need it most seeing what it is saying. It is like they have blinders on when it comes to the subject presented here.

Dr. Parker:

Related to the target audience: 1) Since it seeks to solve the "identity crisis" presently experienced by the Church of Christ, it probably will not be read by many people of other denominations. On the one hand, I feel that many other groups have encountered similar problems and would benefit from such a study. On the other hand, targeting a specific audience is at the same time one of the strengths of your work since it will expose and address problems endemic of our group; and, 2) The manual is designed primarily for groups and you gave your reasons for this decision. I wonder if the manual could to be modified to embrace the needs of the individual as well. To your credit, you stated that the manual could be used by individuals, but that it was not intended for them. I believe in the principle taught by Bonhoeffer's that we must have "a day together" and "a day alone." I find this as well in the Psalms (individual and communal praise and lament). Although a book is not expected to cover all of the bases at once, I do not feel that this is a frivolous matter in your case. After all, in the week between class sessions, your readers will most likely be "alone." Perhaps some sort of daily meditation or method of "finding God in my story" would be helpful for those moments when we are cut out from the group or when we are not a part of a group at all.

Regarding Design: I was curious about the number of sections within the study guide (8 plus prologue and epilogue: = 10 weeks worth of material). You state that this was intended to by used by Sunday school classes and small groups. It seems to me that the manual needs to be expanded to cover at least a quarter's worth of material (at least 12 weeks, if not more).

Regarding Content: Most of the examples given in the manual from Acts are of individual encounters with Jesus (Peter; Paul). I feel that your manual is missing an excellent opportunity to say something positive about Jesus' relationship to his "community." Although focus on the church and its distinctiveness are a part of our problematic past, I feel that we as a community/church need to enter into the story. What is Jesus doing among us now in terms of healing, answering prayers, or giving strength during persecution. I do not feel that the answer to our problems rests solely in finding our "personal identities." We must also find a brand new "institutional identity." I would like to see this addressed at some point. I believe this would add more punch to an already excellent idea.

2. How would you suggest improving the proposed study guide?

Dr. Hicks:

I would like to see a study of ecclesiology in relation to Christology, perhaps using Acts 2:42-47 or some such text. But I think Acts 2 is paradigmatic and it would fit the emphasis on "table fellowship" and community that is in the study guide.

Mr. Hodges:

Does it need to be longer? Eight weeks is a short time. Are there more stories that could be included? Could you go into more detail about how the churches of Christ got where they are now.

Dr. Jones:

I would go ahead, if the market is Churches of Christ, and spell out the modern day equivalent of the issues Jesus was identifying. I'm afraid if the issues of legalism are not spelled out, the very people for whom the study is intended will use the study to judge someone else.

Dr. Parker:

As stated above, I would like to see the manual adapted to take the individual reader into account.

As stated above, add a few more chapters in order to fit the quarter system of a church.

As stated above, address how we can find a new "institutional identity."

3. Speak briefly to the relevance of the proposed study guide both to members of the Church of Christ as well as to the larger Christian community:

Dr. Hicks:

I think my statement above applies to this.

Mr. Hodges:

I think to those church of Christers already struggling with these issues, this study guide will help them to start sorting stuff out. I'm not sure how the larger Christian community would perceive it. Would they understand our issues and agendas of the past? I don't know.

Dr. Jones:

I think all churches have a problem with the identity of Christ, self identity, and legalism. However, the Church of Christ has a unique slant on it with a near cultic mentality on certain issues. To really go for the jugular with the churches of Christ would have to be done with our particular issues or we won't get it. Also churches of Christ have to be separated in an evaluation or they will think it is the other groups that have a problem rather than our group because of our sectarian nature. I think one market or the other needs to be chosen to be effective.

Dr. Parker:

I believe you have put your finger on the problem within the Churches of Christ: i.e., we have an ecclesiology without a Christology. For many years, I have heard the "church" preached in all its glory, whereas Jesus almost seems to be presented as an afterthought. A study guide such as this has the potential of serving as a corrective to this problem.

4. Would you recommend such a study guide to a member of the Church of Christ? Why or why not?

Dr. Hicks:

I think I would, but I would need to see the final product. Looks good at this point.

Mr. Hodges:

Yes I would. I like the approach used and think that a return to discipleship to Christ is the only way our movement or any other will be able to be lights to the world.

Dr. Jones:

Yes. I think that it is the answer. The only hope for the future of the Church of Christ rests within a new identity or perhaps an initial identity with the person of Jesus. I'm really not optimistic that it will accomplish its intent. However, that is not the fault of the study as much as my pessimism about the openness of the movement to the truth of the study.

Dr. Parker:

Before recommending any work to another, I like to read it in its entirety. However, based on the proposal, I do not foresee any reason why I would have reservations about the content and agenda. Although I am in full agreement with the material stated in the section entitled "Inadequacies of the Current Method," it is precisely because of these items that I would exercise caution in freely sharing this material with others. I would recommend this guide to select individuals or to certain elderships, but would also be careful not to cast pearls before swine, lest they turn and rend me.

5. Feel free to share other thoughts regarding the proposed study guide.

Mr. Hodges:

Great job Brad. I would like to see the finished product. I could use it with a few people here I am sure.

Dr. Jones:

I think that in reality the discovery of our problem in the Church of Christ will only happen as a serendipity. And that is what this study does. For instance, you cannot find the answer to a problem on instrumental music by studying instrumental music. However, you can study the identity of Jesus and your problem will be solved. But this doesn't make sense to a person who believes he is justified by being "right" rather than by being "in Christ."

The other thing about the study that would be helpful to me is a greater understanding of how narrative does this. I realize everyone says this and I have also. But I wish that I understood better how narrative can do this. At times it seems like it is just a popular new method. Obviously, this study believes that it is more than method but substantive. I would like to understand this even more than this study or others have given me. I want to be convinced that this shift would be enough when I fear that I need much more.

Thanks for your study.

Reflecting on the Experts' Evaluations

Section One

One is always gratified to have respected Christians express agreement with one's proposals. I am very pleased (and a bit surprised) that my proposal was met with such a positive response by these men for whom I have much adoration. Reading between the lines, however, it is obvious that they held a few reservations. Mr. Hodges agreed, but not strongly, with statements one, two, four, five and six. This suggests that he was a little hesitant to completely endorse the guide as it is proposed. His hesitancies are explicated in his short answers under section two (which I discuss below). For Drs. Hicks, Jones, and Parker the reservations related to their uncertainty over the guide's ability to adequately address the crisis (statements six and seven). These concerns come out in their answers to the questions in section two, and will be addressed next.

Section Two

The experts show no doubt over the existence of the Church of Christ's identity crisis. They also seem generally pleased with the proposal's emphasis on narrative and its potential to address the crisis.

Notwithstanding, they did see some weaknesses in the project. Dr. Hicks is concerned that the study fails to address adequately the need for a new institutional identity. This is counter-balanced by Dr. Parker's desire to see the guide modified to focus even more intentionally upon the individual. My feelings on this are also mixed. While the Church of Christ's future as an institution will require a new corporate identity (especially one that no longer buttresses the present faulty identity of individual Christians), I am not sure this study can risk reaching that far. Churches of Christ are fiercely autonomous; speaking at the institutional level is at best awkward, at worst it is very dangerous. It seems to me that the church's institutional identity will be reshaped from the grassroots. At the same time, I feel it is necessary to work out the issues of personal identity within a community (e.g., small groups and classes). Our tendency toward independent individualism is so strong that I feel confident individuals will read it; I think the challenge will be in getting it into the hands of groups.

Mr. Hodges asks if the problem has been correctly identified. He wonders if our identity crisis is related more to a misunderstanding of the nature of God (one who wants to send us to hell) than to a deficient Christology. My response is that while we do have confusion in our doctrines of God and soteriology, I believe we are best prepared to address them from the standpoint of christo-centric discipleship. I fear that simply attempting to correct our abstract doctrinal misunderstandings will not move us away from our doctrinally-centered identity. The crisis would thus remain.

Dr. Jones worries that those who need the book's message the most will be blind to its implications for them. This legitimate concern dogs the steps of every spiritual reform. For those who have ears to hear, and eyes to see, though, he seems to think the project is promising.

Dr. Parker wonders if the target is too narrow (i.e., the Church of Christ), but concedes that a specific target is necessary for the book to be effective. I agree with him that other denominations have encountered similar problems, I am just not qualified to speak directly to those concerns, as I have spent all my adult life in the Church of Christ.

Drs. Hicks and Parker and Mr. Hodges all suggest that the study should be expanded beyond its current eight-week plan. For Dr. Parker the matter is related to the quarter schedule most Churches of Christ follow. I hear his concern and personally struggle with it as I too must teach within thirteen-week quarters. However, the trend in small group studies appears to be toward an eight-week format. Additionally, there are almost always interruptions in a typical church quarter that keep a teacher from finishing her or his full thirteen-week curriculum. Further, I suspect some class discussions will require more than one class period to resolve. An eight-week study guide gives a teacher flexibility to expand the discussions as needed.

Dr. Hicks sees the need for expansion in order to address the relationship between the church and Christ. I agree that this is an important feature of discipleship, and Dr. Hicks' suggestion that Acts 2:42-47 provides a textual basis for discussing it is valid. In related comments, Mr. Hodges wonders if more needs to be said about how the Churches of Christ got where they are now and Dr. Parker suggests the study guide offers an excellent opportunity to say something positive about Jesus' relationship his community. Perhaps expansion is justified in order to take in these related matters.

Dr. Jones stresses that the study should speak in concrete terms about the issues plaguing the Church of Christ that emerge from our inadequate identity (e.g., legalism). I agree and frankly admit that this side of the study is a bit frightening to me. Having recently experienced a church split, I understand the political risks involved in speaking explicitly about our doctrinal center. Yet, Dr. Jones is correct; abstract theorizing about our problem is hardly remedial.

All four experts show confidence that the study has relevance for members of the Church of Christ, and that its emphasis on narrative is promising. They seem somewhat dubious as to its relevance for the broader Christian community. This reservation seems due more to the need for the study to be specific enough for members of the Church of Christ that they can be challenged by its proposal than due to a weakness in the proposal itself.

When asked if the experts had any addition thoughts to share two did. Mr. Hodges reiterated his approval of the project and suggested that he knew of specific individuals who would be helped by it. Dr. Jones observed that the narrative approach has the benefit of doing its work (reshaping identity) subtly —as a serendipity of looking at the Lukan stories. I appreciate his insight on this point, as that is one of the strongest arguments favoring the use of narrative in preaching and teaching.[30] But Dr. Jones also raises a question concerning the way narrative functions. How does narrative accomplish its purpose? My sense is that the answer he seeks is difficult to nail down precisely. We all have experienced the life-changing influence of stories on our lives, yet do not observe a step-by-step process by which it occurs. I believe narrative does mediate these changes by virtue of the fact that it approximates experience. Good stories so engage us that they generate the sensation of experience. They can even seem more "real" than actual empirical experiences. I will never forget the impact the movie Jaws had on me when I was a teenager. I lived the story so effectively that it was years before I could swim without the fear of a shark attack. Similarly, my reading of John Steinbeck's Travels with Charlie gave me the sense that I had actually visited the foggy coast of Maine and the monumental Redwoods of California. More recently, when I heard Barbara Brown Taylor preach an Epiphany sermon I was so captured by her story that I felt as though I had genuinely gazed upon the baby Jesus along with the Magi. So, while I can appreciate Dr. Jones' curiosity over how story functions in this way, I am satisfied from abundant personal experience that it does. In fact, I am so convinced of it that I guard my daughters from certain stories that would mediate experiences with sin.

Summary and Trajectory

As I reflect on the experts' evaluations I feel greatly encouraged to take the project to the next step —to actually write and seek a publisher for my study guide (I have already begun conversations with someone in the publishing industry). Two of the concerns raised by the experts have caused me to reconsider the length and scope of the study guide. In the first place, while I chose its eight-chapter format on purpose, I admit that expansion may be necessary to accomplish my objectives. In other words, perhaps I should add additional chapters on 1) the cause of the Church of Christ's dilemma; 2) the relationship of disciples with one another; and, 3) the relationship of Christ with the church. Whether this expansion will require five more chapters (and, thus, fill a typical 13-week study) remains to be seen. I won't rule it out, but would prefer shorter over longer.

In the second place, I now wonder whether the study guide should be produced in two different versions (one for the Church of Christ and the other for the broader Christian community). The main benefit of producing two versions is that it would enable me to speak directly to the Church of Christ (with our unique jargon and with pointed examples from our tradition), without alienating a broader audience. If I do produce two different versions, I will seek out the assistance of another minister who has insight into the specific identity issues in other denominations.

As I have developed this project I have at the same time taught classes on Luke-Acts, preached more Lukan stories, and have talked openly about

Christian identity. The experience has been enlightening. I have discovered a general uneasiness about Luke's Jesus —he is, at times, a bit too rough around the edges for upper-middle class Euro-Americans. We wish he would show less interest in marginal peoples and show more appreciation for our personal piety. I have also found that we feel defensive talking about the fact that our identity has a doctrinal center; it is as if we already know that it should be otherwise, but persist with it anyway. The thing that has encouraged me the most, though, has been that by simply telling the stories —and thereby addressing the problem indirectly —people have shown an openness to being reshaped by narrative encounters with Jesus.

NOTES

1 This crisis is being acknowledged by a few Church of Christ writers. The current proposed solutions involve a rethinking of ecclesiology. For two important examples, see Shelly (1992) and Hughes (1995).

2 These phrases serve as identity-marking slogans for the Church of Christ.

3 All Scripture citations are from the New Revised Standard Version of the Bible, copyright 1989.

4 Although it might sound as though Christians are people who exchanged their identity for the identity of Jesus Christ, this is incorrect. The identity that emerges from the collision of my story with the story of Jesus Christ is uniquely mine. I do not take the place of Jesus in the world--I take my place as a disciple of Jesus whose life is led by the same Spirit as was his. "Following Jesus means following the Spirit; identifying with Jesus means having a Christian identity" (Christian Doquoc:132). After all,

The wind blows where it wills, and you hear the sound of it, but you do not know whence it comes or whither it goes; so it is with everyone who is born of the Spirit. . .

The Spirit has not been commissioned to repeat ad infinitum what happened once. His task is to get rid of that kind of imitation so that each person can win through to his or her identity. Jesus would not have asked people to part from their father, from their mother, from their brothers and sisters, and from their wife, in order to put himself in their place by reinforcing the bonds of dependence. Imitating Jesus means attaining in the Spirit to a comparable freedom, to an analogous love to which no one can take some commonplace route, for it is unique. (Duquoc: 132)

5 Much of Reimarus' work remained unpublished until after his death. It was Gotthold Lessing who, between the years 1774 and 1778, published excerpts of Reimarus' writings.

6 There is no consensus regarding the distinction between the second and third quests. This discussion follows the scheme outlined by N.T. Wright. Other scholars, such as Leander Keck, see the Jesus Seminar as representative of the third quest.

7 Thirty-seven "rules of evidence" were formulated by the fellows to evaluate each saying's authenticity (Funk:19-36). It is clear that the particular type of Jesus found, was the one that was intentionally sought (see Richard B. Hays, "The Corrected Jesus" First Things, May 1994, 43-48; Howard Clark Kee, "A Century of Quests for the Culturally Compatible Jesus" Theology Today, April 1995, 17-28).

8 Other names associated with the third quest include: B.F. Meyers, A.E. Harvey, Marcus Borg, et al.

9 This approach may also be broader in scope and begin with the nature of deity (from above) or the nature of humanity (from below). Hence, a "from below" approach might start with a general study of anthropology, then move to Jesus as a human who partook of the universals of humanity. Or, this approach may examine the humanity of Jesus and view his life as the model of true humanity.

10 Although this paradigm has roots in the patristic age, the contemporary scholars most commonly associated with the approach "from below" are Wolfhart Pannenberg, Karl Rahner, Hans Küng, Edward Schillebeeckx.

11 This interpretation based upon a synthesis of the material found in Leroy Garrett (The Stone-Campbell Movement. Joplin, MO: College Press, 1981), Nathan Hatch (The Democratization of American Christianity. New Haven, CT: Yale University Press, 1991), Sidney E. Alhstrom (A Religious History of the American People. New Haven, CT: Yale University Press, 1972) and personal observation.

12 Sidney Alhstrom has said: "literal allegiance to Alexander Campbell's program for transcending Christian division resulted in one of America's most robust examples of rigorous exclusivism" (823).

13 See Crites (74-76).

14 Of course, this also opens the door for us to attempt to deceive a new acquaintance by coloring our story in a dishonest manner. Yet, once the individual learns more of our story (over time and through experience) the deception becomes difficult to maintain.

15 Modernism's obituary is being written by a growing number of scholars (see Stanley J. Grenz A Primer on Postmodernism. Grand Rapids: Eerdmans, 1996; Diogenes Allen, et al. Postmodern Theology:

Christian Faith in a Pluralistic World. San Francisco: Harper & Row, 1989 et al.).

16 See Crossan (1981:13).

17 Elizabeth Barnes builds on Lindbeck's The Nature of Doctrine: Religion and Theology in a Postliberal Age (Philadelphia: Westminster Press, 1984) in her discussion of the role of narrative in discipleship.

18 I well remember the tears that filled my eyes when I read Craddock's sermon "Praying Through Clenched Teeth" (Lowry:148). This epiphany occurred while I was a student under Dr. Lucy Rose (Narrative Preaching, CTS January 1994).

19 See MacIntyre (89-110).

20 Robert Alter (The Art of Biblical Narrative) and V. Philips Long (The Art of Biblical History) and Robert Tannehill (The Narrative Unity of Luke-Acts) are among the growing number of scholars who are beginning to bring to light the fruits of studying the narrative portions of Scripture from a Narrative-Critical approach.

21 Words from the song "Amazing Grace" by John Newton (1779).

22 "The metaphor of `collision' is appropriate for describing this encounter because in many instances if a person's identity is illumined and transformed by the Christian faith, if revelation takes place, significant disorientation and reinterpretation take place" (Stroup:95).

23 I'll never forget the sense of crisis I felt when confronted with the possibility that the Lord's Supper could be eaten on a day other than Sunday. The "Sunday only" doctrine was so engrained in me that to suggest it could be eaten on another day was tantamount, it seemed to me, to no longer being a Christian.

24 Of course, from the biblical perspective, this transformation is never completely achieved—it is ongoing (see Philippians 3:12-16).

25 Stroup defines self-deception as "a discrepancy between the past and what a person says about the past, and an incoherence between how a person actually lives in the world and the account that person offers to others" (1997:127). For David, the discrepancy was in his acting as though he was still righteous in spite of his unrighteousness.

26 The self-deception was shattered when challenged by a member of David's community. According to Stroup, "It may be that self-deception is recognized for what it is only when a person is called to some form of accounting by another person or by a community" (129).

27 In the mythical world of Star Trek: The Next Generation (a TV and motion picture series) there is a race of humanoids called the Borg. This race has eliminated individuality and all its members are simply drones that operate as part of a "collective." This is not a biblical model for the church.

28 Campbell has a useful, sustained discussion of the role of community in hermeneutics (221-257).

29 It is unclear whether Jesus was asserting knowledge of his unique relationship with the heavenly Father, or simply speaking with childish literalism about his developing understanding of his Jewish faith (as a son of the law).

30 This is what Fred Craddock refers to as "overhearing the Gospel" (Craddock:1978).

BIBLIOGRAPHY

Achtemeier, Paul J.

1992 "Gospel of Mark." The Anchor Bible Dictionary, ed. David Noel Freedman. New York: Doubleday. IV:541-557.

Alhstrom, Sidney E.

1972 A Religious History of the American People. New Haven, CT: Yale University Press.

Allen, Diogenes, et al.

1989 Postmodern Theology: Christian Faith in a Pluralistic World. San Francisco: Harper & Row.

Alter, Robert

1981 The Art of Biblical Narrative. San Francisco: Basic Books.

Barnes, Elizabeth

1995 The Story of Discipleship: Christ, Humanity, and the Church in Narrative Perspective. Nashville: Abingdon Press.

Borg, Marcus

1994 "Profiles in Scholarly Courage: Early Days of New Testament Criticism," Bible Review 105:40-45.

Bühler, Pierre

1988 "Christian Identity: Between Objectivity and Subjectivity." in Christian Identity. edited by Christian Duquoc and Casiano Floristán. Edinburgh: T&T Clark LTD.

Campbell, Charles L.

1997 Preaching Jesus: New Directions for Homiletics in Hans Frei's Postliberal Theology. Grand Rapids: Eerdmans.

Craddock, Fred

1978 Overhearing the Gospel: Preaching and Teaching the Faith to Persons Who Have Already Heard. Nashville: Abingdon Press.

Crites, Stephen

1971 "The Narrative Quality of Experience." in Why Narrative? Readings in Narrative Theology. Edited by Stanley Hauerwas and L. Gregory Jones. 1997. Eugene, OR: Wipf & Stock Publishers.

Crossan, John Dominic

1994 Jesus: A Revolutionary Biography. San Francisco: HarperSanFrancisco.

1988 The Dark Interval: Towards a Theology of Story. Sonoma, CA: Polebridge Press.

Duquoc, Christian

1988 Christian Identity. Edinburgh: T&T Clark LTD.

Dupuis, Jacques

1994 Who Do You Say I Am: Introduction to Christology. Maryknoll, NY: Orbis Books.

Frei, Hans W.

1975 The Identity of Jesus Christ. Philadelphia: Fortress.

Foreman, Kenneth Joseph

1963 Identification: Human and Divine. Richmond, VA: John Knox Press.

Fuller, Reginald H. and Pheme Perkins

1983 Who Is This Christ? Philadelphia: Fortress.

Funk, Robert, et al.

1993 The Five Gospels: The Search for the Authentic Words of Jesus. New York: Macmillan Publishing Company.

Garrett, Leroy

1981 The Stone-Campbell Movement. Joplin, MO: College Press.

Green, Joel B.

1995 The Theology of The Gospel of Luke. Cambridge: University Press.

Grenz, Stanley J.

1996 A Primer on Postmodernism. Grand Rapids: Eerdmans.

Guelich, Robert A.

1991 "The 'Christ' of the Gospel: A Lesson from Mark's Christology" in Perspectives On Christology: Essays in Honor of Paul K. Jewett. eds. Marguerite Shuster and Richard Muller. Grand Rapids: Zondervan.

Guthrie, Shirley C.

1994 Christian Doctrine Revised Edition. Louisville: Westminster/John Knox Press.

Hatch, Nathan

1991 The Democratization of American Christianity. New Haven, CT: Yale University Press.

Hays, Richard B.

1994 "The Corrected Jesus" First Things. May, pp. 43-48.

Hilkert, Mary Catherine

1997 Naming Grace: Preaching and the Sacramental Imagination. New York: Continuum.

Hughes, Richard T.

1995 "Reclaiming a Heritage." Restoration Quarterly (37:3).

1996 Reviving the Ancient Faith: The Story of Churches of Christ in America. Grand Rapids: Eerdmans.

Hyppolytus

nd Refutation of All Heresies. Book 7:22. Book 8:1-4.

Ignatius

nd To the Philadelphians. Chapter 6.

Irenaeus

nd Against Heresies. Chapter 15; 26.

Johnson, Luke Timothy

1992 "The Book of Luke-Acts." The Anchor Bible Dictionary, ed. David Noel Freedman. New York: Doubleday. IV:403-420.

1996 The Real Jesus: The Misguided Quest for the Historical Jesus and the Truth of the Traditional Gospels. San Francisco: HarperSanFrancisco.

Kähler, Martin

1964 The So-called Historical Jesus and the Historic Biblical Christ. Philadelphia: Fortress Press.

Kant, Immanuel

1784 "What is Enlightenment?" in The Philosophy of Kant: Immanuel Kant's Moral and Political Writings. Edited by Carl J. Friedrich. New York: The Modern Library, 1949.

Kysar, Robert

1992 "Gospel of John." The Anchor Bible Dictionary, ed. David Noel Freedman. New York: Doubleday. III:912-931.

Long, V. Philips

1994 The Art of Biblical History. Grand Rapids, MI: Zondervan Publishing House.

Lowry, Eugene

1989 How to Preach A Parable: Designs for Narrative Sermons. Nashville: Abingdon Press.

Mack, Burton L.

1993 The Lost Gospel: The Book of Q & Christian Origins. San Francisco: HarperSanFrancisco.

MacIntyre, Alasdair

1981 "The Vitues, the Unity of a Human Life, and the Concept of a Tradition." in Why Narrative? Readings in Narrative Theology. Edited by Stanley Hauerwas and L. Gregory Jones. 1997. Eugene, OR: Wipf & Stock Publishers.

Macquarrie, John

1990 Jesus Christ in Modern Thought. Philadelphia: Trinity Press.

Meier, John P.

1992 "Gospel of Matthew." The Anchor Bible Dictionary, ed. David Noel Freedman. New York: Doubleday. IV:622-641.

Moltmann, Jürgen

1990 The Way of Jesus Christ: Christology in Messianic Dimensions. Minneapolis: Fortress.

O'Collins, Gerald

1995 Christology: A Biblical, Historical, and Systematic Study of Jesus Christ. Oxford: Oxford University Press.

Ostling, Richard N.

1994 "Jesus Christ, Plain and Simple." Time January 10.

Overman, J. Andrew

1990 Matthew's Gospel and Formative Judaism: The Social World of the Matthean Community. Minneapolis: Fortress Press.

Pannenberg, Wolfhart

1977 Jesus, God and Man. Philadelphia: Westminster.

Percival, Henry R.

1899 "The Seven Ecumenical Councils of the Undivided Church" in The Nicene and Post-Nicene Fathers (reprint 1973). Grand Rapids: Eerdmans.

Runia, Klaas

1984 The Present-Day Christological Debate. Downers Grove: InterVarsity.

Sanders, E.P.

1993 The Historical Figure of Jesus. London: Penguin Books.

Shelly, Rubel and Randall J. Harris

1992 The Second Incarnation: A Theology for the 21st Century Church. West Monroe: Howard Publishing Company.

Strimple, Robert B.

1995 The Modern Search for the Real Jesus. Philipsburg: P&R Publishing.

Stroup, George W.

1997 The Promise of Narrative Theology. Eugene, OR: Wipf & Stock Publishers.

Tannehill, Robert C.

1986 The Narrative Unity of Luke-Acts: A Literary Interpretation Volume 1: The Gospel According to Luke. Philadelphia: Fortress Press.

Tiede, David L.

1988 Augsburg Commentary on the New Testament: Luke. Minneapolis, MN: Augsburg Publishing House.

Troeltsch, Ernst

1898 "Historical and Dogmatic Method in Theology" in Religion in History (1991 reprint). Minneapolis: Fortress.

Watson, Russell

1994 "A Lesser Child of God." Newsweek April 4.

Willard, Dallas

1998 The Divine Conspiracy: Rediscovering Our Hidden Life in God. San Francisco: HaperSanFrancisco.

Wright, N.T.

1992 Who Was Jesus? Grand Rapids: Eerdmans.

www.ingramcontent.com/pod-product-compliance
Ingram Content Group UK Ltd.
Pitfield, Milton Keynes, MK11 3LW, UK
UKHW041934190726
13854UKWH00004B/1582

9 781329 775213